12-95

To Paul & Lucille
from Tom & Lori

"me 'n Mama"

Delores Swan

Walter's wife and helpmeet.

"me 'n Mama"

How We Raised Eight Kids
and Survived

Written by
Walter Swan and Deloris Swan

This book is dedicated
to our children,
and other family members
for their great love
and support, without
which we wouldn't be
where we are today.
And to the many dear
friends, old and new,
who have encouraged
and supported us.

CONTENTS

FOREWORD

One of the nice things about writing, putting your own book together and publishing it, is that you can do it anyway you want to without having to follow all the "established rules", whether it's right or wrong. It makes it a lot more fun, too.

This book has been written at the request of many, many people who have read our book, *"me 'n Henry"*. They tell us that we have left them hanging in the air. They want to know: "What happened to your mother and father? Is Henry still alive? Where did you meet Deloris? What happened in California? When did you come back to Arizona?" And so on, and so on. With *"me 'n Mama", How We Raised Eights Kids And Survived*, we hope to be able to answer some of your questions.

Some of these stories will overlap a little in the time sequence. We're sorry about that, but we can't stop in the middle of one story to tell another one.

We are finding that there is so much to put into this book that it would be too long and you might get bored before you got to the end of it. We don't want you to do that. So we'll be writing another one to follow this one, which we plan to title *"me 'n Grandma", How We Spent Our Kids Inheritance*.

We are having fun putting this book together. It is helping the two of us to increase our love for each other because in looking back, we are appreciating each other more and more.

When Walter is doing the story telling it will be in this typeface. *When Deloris is is doing the story telling it will be in this typeface.*

We have found that our lives are constantly turning from one direction to another by the decisions that we make, some of them very small and seemingly insignificant and sometimes major ones.

We did some very stupid things in ignorance which we look back on, almost in horror at our stupidity. But some how we all survived. It hasn't been easy, but it's been worth it.

We hope you enjoy our stories.

Walter and Deloris

PREFACE

THE SWANS

These are the Swans
And how they grew.
Their growth and development
Is pictured here, too.

Jerry and Jim, twins #1
Were the first ones in line.
Charlotte Elizabeth
Followed closely behind.

Carol Ann came
In the year '45.
Three years later,
Allen did arrive.

John and Merri Lou, twins #2,
Were next in line, you see.
They were followed soon after
By Linda Lee.

They've grown up together
And had lots of fun.
They're closely united
And live just as one.

Their pleasures and highlights
Are here in this book.
They're carefully recorded
By the pictures we took.

It's taken many years
To gather these scenes.
There's been laughter and tears
Betwixt and between.

We thought you'd enjoy
A peek here and there
Our pleasures and joys
We want you to share.

When you arrive
At the end of this book,
Return to this page
And take another look.

But this isn't the end
Of the Swan's history.
We'll be adding more and more
From here to eternity.

Chapter One

IT WAS LOVE AT FIRST SIGHT

It happened fifty-three years ago, on Friday, April 19, 1940 to be exact, in the basement of the First Baptist Church in Stockton, California. I was twenty-three and she was almost nineteen.

I was invited to a dinner social put on by the college-age young men and women. It was one of those kinds of affairs that was the end of some kind of a contest where the losers had to cook the meal for the winners, then eat beans while the winners ate turkey. I can't remember whether I ate beans or turkey, but I do remember that pretty young lady who was waiting tables.

As she came to our table I said to my brother, who was also a guest, "See that girl, Henry? That's her! She is the one I've been waiting for all of my life. I am going to marry her some day!"

Of course, this remark brought the response, "How are you going to do that?"

I said, "Well, if you want something bad enough, you will find a way to do it."

These were the thoughts that went through my mind – Walter, you can't possibly do this. Why, you don't know anything about that girl. How can this ever take place? You are just fresh off the range. What you know about girls wouldn't help you a bit. You don't even know how to talk to a girl. She doesn't even know you. But I made up my mind that I wanted her for my wife.

I didn't see her again for three weeks, then my opportunity came when this same group of young people had a very early morning picnic on Saturday, May 11th at one of the local parks to make up for the beans some of them had to eat at their first social.

This same girl was there! I made the opportunity to talk with her during the time we were there at the picnic. I introduced myself and learned that her name was Deloris Robinson. She had come to the picnic with her brother, Don, and his girl friend in their folks Model A Ford.

It was along about 10:30 in the morning when everybody was getting ready to go home. Deloris' brother wasn't ready to go home right then 'cause he wanted to go over to his girl friend's house for a while. Deloris wanted to go home. I couldn't help over hearing their conversation.

Oh, how I wished I had a car at this time. But that did not stop me! The only means of transportation that I had was my blue bicycle with balloon tires. I stepped up and offered to take her home on my bicycle and she accepted! Now was my big chance! That is, if I didn't blow it.

I didn't know that it was eight miles and clear across town to her home. It took us about two hours or more to get to her house. She sat kinda side-saddle-like on the frame between the handle bars and the seat. I put my feet on the pedals and we were off! My feet and legs didn't even feel the extra weight of having her there so close to me with my arms almost around her. I was a-ridin' on cloud nine!

All of the way to her house I was a-tellin' her about my philosophies of life, and, among other things, I told her what I thought a wife should be and what a husband should be and she listened patiently.

About half way there she was beginning to get pretty uncomfortable so I stopped and took off my sleeveless green sweater that my mother had knitted for me and gave it to her to sit on. (She didn't tell me till I got to know her a lot better that she got a big bruise on her hip about the size of a grapefruit from bumping against the point of the bicycle seat.)

When we got there I was pretty thirsty so she made me a big tall ice-cold glass of lemonade. Boy, did it taste good! It was the best lemonade I ever tasted in my life. Then she fixed me a big bowl of strawberries with good thick fresh cream on them and they were the best straw berries I ever ate in my life.

The next Monday I heard a faint knock on the front door of my rooming house. My land lady, Mrs. Bennett, answered the door. It sounded like a young woman a-talkin' to her and I heard my name mentioned. I hurried out to see who it was and there was Deloris! She had my green sweater. I had left it at her house and she was bringing it back.

I invited her into my room. (Mrs. Bennett didn't like the idea too much, but she went away a-mumblin' under her breath.) We talked for a little while and I gave Deloris a small sweater lapel pin that my mother had knitted for me, and I got her phone number so I could call her. She couldn't stay long 'cause she was on her lunch hour. She was going to school a-learnin' how to be an office worker.

The next day I called her, and the next, and the next. Then on Friday she called me! She was inviting me to go to Sacramento with her and her church group to a Baptist youth rally.

She explained to me that she had invited a little short guy to go to the rally, but he had gotten the idea that she was inviting him to go with her. She said she needed some "protection". She didn't like him and she didn't want him to get the idea that she did. I said that I would go with her.

Well, when we all gathered to load up the cars for the trip, we ended up with three couples for Don's car. Don and his girlfriend sat in the front seat and Deloris sat up there with them. Vincent and Jean sat in the back seat. I had to sit back with them. I wasn't too happy about that, but when we got to the rally, I sat beside Deloris.

When the rally was over and we got into the car, I suggested that Deloris sit on my lap for the trip home. It was a fifty mile trip, but she didn't object! I must have been a-doin' something right!

About half-way home we had a flat tire. While Don changed it, Deloris and I took a little stroll down the highway in the moonlight. She invited me to come over for Sunday dinner the next day. I said I would if she cooked the dinner. She said she would and I accepted her invitation. Things were a-gettin' better all the time.

When we got back to Stockton, Don dropped off Jean and Vincent, then Mary Ellen at their homes. I was the last one. By this time I sure wanted to kiss her, but I didn't dare, especially with her brother there.

The next day, I went to church for the first time in my life.

We had planned a bicycle ride for me and Deloris, and Don and Mary Ellen after dinner, so I borrowed another bicycle and Deloris' other brother and I rode them out to the Robinson's house. On the way, Lee got in my way and I fell off my bicycle in

3

the middle of the street. I had a roll of 35 mm. film in my shirt pocket and I broke a rib when I landed on it. Now I was a-hurtin' pretty bad, but we made it home okay.

That day I found out that she could cook. We had fried chicken with all the trimmings. That home cookin' sure did taste good. And we had a FUN day!

The first picture I took of Deloris

Let me back up our story a little here to that fateful day, Friday, April 19th. I was on the losing side of that church dinner, so I went to the church in the morning to help prepare it. Mrs. Robinson (not a relative) was the cook in charge.

I was grating carrots for the salad when Mrs. Robinson asked me to go outside and give Irvin Grubbs a message. Irvin was outside because he was freezing the ice cream the good old-fashioned way.

He wasn't alone! There was a very tall, lanky, handsome, young man standing there talking to him. Irvin introduced us. His name was Walter Swan.

I delivered the message and we talked for a few minutes, then I went back into the kitchen and continued with my carrot grating.

A little later I looked up and there stood Walter taking a picture of me. I couldn't understand why he wanted a picture of me when we had just met each other. We talked for a little while, then he left.

That evening he showed up for the dinner with his brother, Henry, as guests of Irvin. I don't remember paying too much attention to them that night, and I didn't see Walter again until three weeks later.

About 5:00 a.m. on that next fateful day, Saturday, May 11th, Walter showed up on his pretty blue Schwinn bicycle with balloon tires at Victory Park where we were to meet and ride bicycles over to Lewis Park, a distance of two or three miles.

When we got there, the youth leaders were preparing our breakfast. We all ate, played games, and had a good time. Walter seemed to want to talk more than play, so we visited quite a lot while we were there.

About 10:30 everyone started to go home. I had a date with my boyfriend that evening and I was anxious to get home so I could get my hair washed and get ready for my date, but Don had other plans. When Walter said he'd take me home on his bicycle I accepted his invitation.

The next Wednesday, one of the girls in our youth group was having a birthday party. I invited Walter to go with me. Don wasn't going this time, so I drove the Model A Ford over and picked up Walter. We had a good time at the party and I drove him back to his rooming house.

We sat outside and talked for a little while. He told me that he could care for me very much and asked me if I thought I could care for him. I had told him about my boyfriend, but he didn't let that bother him any. I told him that I would let him know as soon as I knew and he kissed me before I left him. Since we were sitting side by side, he missed my mouth by a little, but it was a kiss I would never forget.

The next Sunday, he went to church and came out for dinner again, and we went to the Sunday evening meetings, too. This time he drove his old broken down car and took me home in it. When we

5

got to my house we sat in the car talking. It seemed the more we talked, the more we wanted to talk. By that time I had decided that I could care for him and I told him so. This was cause for more talking, and we were getting happier and happier.

I was so happy that I wanted to share the good news about Vincent and Jean who were planning to announce their engagement at the May 30th "retreat" our youth group was having up at Mt. Diablo and I told him about it even though I was supposed to keep it a secret.

Then he said, "How about me 'n you announcing our engagement at the same time?"

I was flabbergasted!

"Do you mean that?" I asked excitedly.

"Of course I mean it."

"Oh, Walter! Yes! Yes!" I cried.

About that time I got a _real_ kiss!

About midnight my mother came out to the car and said that she thought it was time for me to come into the house, that I had been sitting out there too long talking to a man I didn't know very well. I told her that Walter had just asked me to marry him.

She must have assumed that my answer was yes because she just said, "Oh!" and turned around and went back into the house. She never asked me to come into the house again.

That day was May 26, 1940, five weeks after we had first seen each other.

The next day Walter came over with a diamond ring for me. _Now_ we really had a lot to talk about, and we did, until about midnight or so every night.

I don't know how Walter managed to work the next day after staying up so late every night. He was working for the California State Highway Department chopping the weeds from around the oleanders along the state highways. It was very hot out there in the summer sun, but he didn't seem to mind.

We set our marriage date for August 30th, my parents twenty first wedding anniversary. That was three months away. Later, we decided that was just too far away. The more time we spent together, the more we loved each other. So we changed the date to July 4th because Walter would have a four day holiday and we planned to go up to the mountains and camp out for our honeymoon.

Chapter Two

DELORIS' BACKGROUND

Before we go any further in this story, I guess we ought to give you a little background on me. (You've already read about Walter's childhood.)

My name is Deloris (spelled D-E-L-O-R-I-S) Cavell Robinson Swan. I am probably the only person who has ever lived or will ever live with that exact name. I was born in Merced, California on June 30, 1921. I have two younger brothers, Charles Donald (Don), born in 1922 and Leland Ray (Lee) born in 1924. We were raised in a good Christian home.

My father was George Ray Robinson, born in West Virginia in 1899. Dad lived to be ninety-one years old. My mother is Charlotte Tessie Page Robinson, born in Missouri in 1903. Mom is still alive and is ninety years old. They both lived to celebrate their seventy-first wedding anniversary. Both of my parents are mainly of English stock. I have many ancestors who lived to be in their late eighties or early nineties.

Dad worked for the Atchison, Topeka, and Santa Fe Railway Company for thirty-five years as a telegraph lineman. We never suffered during the Great Depression like Walter and many other people did because Dad worked all the way through it, although we did lose some money in the bank closures.

During those thirty-five years he was transferred quite a number of times, so moving to new places was something we did without question. He first worked as a lineman in Fresno, California when I was five or six years old. Right after we moved to Winslow, Arizona I had my seventh birthday. We lived in Needles, California during the year I was ten, then back to Winslow a few days before my eleventh birthday.

Dad always wanted to be a farmer, so in 1933 we made a trip to California and my folks found a twenty acre piece of farming land

7

near Oakdale, which they bought. For two years Dad made plans to move there as soon as we could. He spent many hours drawing house plans and plot plans for our farm.

After saving up for the move for two years, he stripped down the old 1925 Star touring car we had, and made a small pickup truck with it. Then he packed everything he could into it. Mom and Dad put "us kids" on the train by ourselves to go to Le Grand, California to stay with our paternal grandparents until they were ready at the farm for us. We celebrated my fourteenth and Don's thirteenth birthday that month.

Dad took a thirty-day leave without pay. (Paid vacations were unheard of in those days.) We camped in a tent while we helped him build a temporary house which was to be used as a garage later.

Dad was never able to set aside quite enough money to make the change over from working for the Santa Fe to being an independent farmer. He tried for three years while Mom, my brothers and I lived in Oakdale where I went to high school.

I graduated from Oakdale High School on June 3, 1938 before my seventeenth birthday. The next day we moved to Stockton where Dad had been transferred a few months before.

That fall I went to the Stockton Junior College for one school year. I took English Composition and Accounting – never knowing at the time that those courses would be very valuable to me in later years. The next year I took a post graduate business course in the Schnieder Vocational High School where I learned typing, shorthand, and business machines.

That's where I was when I met Walter and it didn't take long for the direction of my life to change dramatically.

Deloris' Senior High School Picture

The Robinsons: Ray, Deloris, Lee, Charlotte, Don

Chapter Three

ME 'N DELORIS GOT MARRIED

It was the third day of July 1940 and the BIG DAY was a-comin' up on the fourth. All of the plans had been made for the wedding at eight in the morning in the First Baptist Church on Hunter St.

Here I was, all alone in this rooming house just a-waiting till tomorrow got here and that seemed like an eternity. I didn't even have a clock. When I wanted to find out what time it was, all I did was to go next door to the service station on the corner. There was a big clock up on the wall, and it could be seen from the street.

I sat on the front porch hoping to see someone that I knew walk by. But that didn't happen, so I just sat outside for a long time a-dreaming of our life together and if the rest of it was as good as the first was, I wanted to be with her forever. I didn't care how hard it was to make a living or what anybody else thought. This is what I wanted and now it was going to be a-happenin' in just a little while.

Then I wondered if all of the young men felt this way just before they got married. Sometimes I felt as if I was a-floating in space and wasn't sure that it was really happening to me.

There was a full moon out that night and it even out-shined the street light. How I wished there was someone there to share these wonderful feelings with. Then the thought went through my mind, this is the last night that I will ever be a bachelor.

The moon was up in the sky about ten o'clock high by now and it was time to go to bed and get a good rest for the big day tomorrow. It was pretty warm and there was no cooler at all in that room, so I just laid there on top of the bed and tried to go to sleep. But I was afraid to go to sleep for fear I might not wake up in time for the wedding.

After a little, I dozed off, then woke up with a start. I just knew it would start to get light pretty soon so I laid there for a long time a-waitin'. Finally, I got up and put on all of my clothes and sat on the edge of the bed and looked out the window.

I said, "Well, I'll go and look and see what time that clock at the station says." But when I looked at it, it was only twelve thirty and I couldn't believe it. So I took another look at the moon and according to moon time that clock was right. So I went back to bed. That was the longest night that I ever spent in my whole life I do believe. I stopped a-countin' how many times I got up and put on my clothes to go see what time it was.

Well, it was finally day break and I showered and shaved what few whiskers there was on my upper lip. The rest of my face was so soft and free from whiskers that it embarrassed me. A man old enough to get married should have a beard.

Then my mind became a total blank. I don't remember a thing I till was a-standing in front of all those people in the church and seeing my wife-to-be a-walking down the isle with her father.

She sure looked pretty! Why in the world would such a pretty girl want to marry someone like me I asked myself. Then I got real scared and was about to start crying, but I choked it back. Then the preacher of the First Baptist Church in Stockton, California, Rev. F. Carl Truex, stood in front of us and it was all over in just a few minutes. I kissed my little wife and we started for the door. We went out the door and got into the car and drove home.

This was the first wedding that I ever went to and I didn't know what I was supposed to do. Years later, I learned that a lot of the wedding presents people brought, they took them back home with them 'cause we didn't stay around to shake their hands. But this didn't bother me in the least 'cause I was married to the sweetest little girl in the world and that is all that mattered.

The evening before we were to get married, we had a wedding rehearsal. There wasn't much to do because we were having an early morning wedding and everything would be simple. My family took me home early, about 8:30 or 9:00.

I sure did miss Walter. We had been with each other every evening until midnight or later since he had proposed to me. I didn't know what to do with myself. But the time eventually passed and we were at the church early in the morning, Thursday, July 4, 1940.

Our wedding was scheduled for 8:00 a.m. We arrived early because we had to sign the marriage license and have some pictures taken. Henry, Walter's brother and best man, and Margaret Thorpe, my bridesmaid, were there in time to sign as witnesses and be in some of the pictures.

It wasn't long until it was time to start. My brother, Don, sang Because*, then I was walking down the isle with my father. The sun was shining through the stained glass windows on the east side of the room causing a beautiful glow throughout the whole chapel. And there at the front, was Walter, smiling at me and looking as if his heart would burst.*

I don't remember much of the ceremony, but I do remember that when it was over, we kissed a long, loving kiss. In fact, it was so long that the congregation began to snicker, so we decided we'd better stop.

Walter had been worried about someone messing up our car so he had his step-father, Ray Boyer, waiting outside the door to pick us up and take us to our new little house. We'd go back later and get our car.

Nobody told us that we were supposed to stand at the back of the chapel and shake hands with all the people who attended our wedding. We had asked the preacher to announce that we would have a reception at our house at one o'clock in the afternoon.

When we felt that everyone had left the church, we had Ray, take us back to the church to pick up our own car.

It was the fourth of July. The parade would be starting at 11:00 a.m. so we went down town and watched the parade and had lunch at the Silver Leaf where we had shared our very first lunch together. We could buy a hamburger and a milkshake for twenty-five cents. That was our first meal as Mr. and Mrs. Walter James Swan.

Then we went back to our new little house to wait for our reception guests. Only a few showed up. I guess they weren't very happy about our leaving the church without shaking hands with them. I don't blame them a bit. Besides, it was a holiday and everyone had something else they wanted to do.

But I didn't care. I was married to the most wonderful man in the world! It had been exactly two and a half months since we had first laid eyes on each other.

Mr. and Mrs. Walter James Swan

Henry, Walter, Deloris, and Margaret

The newlyweds over the threshold
of their new honeymoon cottage.

Chapter Four

OUR FIRST HOME

It was about 8:30 a.m. after we were married that we were heading for the new two-room house that we had rented for fifteen dollars a month, and that included all of the utilities. It was a little house in the neighbor's backyard. There was a path to a very small square building with a Sears catalog in it. (In other words, it was an outdoor toilet.) But we were so much in love that we didn't mind at all. What we wanted was to be together.

On the way home, we kept a-lookin' back to see if there was any one a-followin' us. We had a pretty good start on them if they did get any notions like that. We didn't have any old cans or old shoes tied to the back of the car, anyway. I felt good about this. I felt like getting married was a sacred and wonderful thing and it was not nice to bother a couple after they were married. They already had a lot to contend with without all of those extra things to worry about.

We pulled up in front of our new house. It was just off of Waterloo Road not very far from the Waterloo Cannery. I carried Deloris into the house and we both sat down and looked at each other and smiled.

I said, "Now we are man and wife." And I reached over and held her hand and just looked at her for the longest time. In my mind I had vision of what we would do together and all of the happiness we would have together with a house full of little kids, a milk cow, a big garden and a good job.

A job! When I thought of that it put a cold feeling up my spine 'cause at that time my job working for the state highway department, which had been a-payin' me one hundred dollars a month, was about to play out. I had no money, that is, except for fifteen dollars in my pocket, but I shrugged it off by saying to myself, who needs money when they are in love?

We figured that all we had better do was to hold hands, 'cause who knows, we might be a-havin' a lot of company in a little while.

The house had a wonderful smell to it. It was a new house and no one had lived in it before. You could smell the new wood just like it came out of the forest. Even today the smell of new wood makes my heart skip a beat and puts me in mind of this first day that we were married.

There was not a lot of furniture, just the bare necessities. There was a bed, a table and chairs, a dresser, an ice box (not a refrigerator), and a kitchen stove, all borrowed, and that was about it. We did have some dishes, pots and pans, and some linens.

Our new home had two rooms, each about eleven feet by twelve feet. Each room had an outside door opening onto a small porch on the same side of the house with a small unfinished and unusable bathroom between the two porches.

We used one room for the kitchen and dining room and the other, we used for the bedroom. There was no living room so we used either room for that purpose according to whether we had company or not. The floor was pine flooring, with no carpets or linoleum. The windows had no curtains so we had to improvise in order to cover them.

We had planned our wedding for the fourth of July because Walter would have a four day holiday, since the fourth fell on a Thursday. We wanted to go on a camping trip up in the mountains somewhere.

BUT, Walter got sick with the flu about two or three weeks before we were to be married. He had to take several days off from work, so when he got his paycheck just before we got married, it was way too short for any frivolous spending like that.

We hadn't laid in a supply of groceries and needed household supplies, so the next day we went to the Stockton Consumer's Co-op that Irvin Grubbs managed and where Henry worked. We still have the grocery tickets.

This is what we bought:
First ticket:

Ant powder	.07
Matches	.08
Salt	.08
Mayonnaise	.38

3 cans corn 26
3 cans peas 25
Pepper 05
1 can kidney beans 10
2 cans tomato juice 35
Babette 19
2 lb. American cheese 51
10 lbs. sugar 52
Cornmeal 31
10 lbs. flour 45
Baking powder 19
Total 3.75
Second ticket:
Wheat cereal 19
Dutch cleanser 07
Ant baiter 15
Crackers 29
Toothpaste 21
4 cans milk 25
2 cans Dainty Mix 23
2 cans vegetable mix 28
Wax paper 15
4 cucumbers 08
1 head lettuce 05
1 head celery 10
1 bunch carrots 04
Tomatoes 05
Sweet pickles 25
Total 6.14

Third ticket:
1 lb. butter 35
½ lb. bacon 15
Shoe polish 10
Lemons 12
Grapefruit 10
Grapenuts 13
1 loaf bread 08
3 lbs. Spry (shortening) 49

```
4 ears corn . . . . . . . . . . . . . . . . . . . . . . . .12
Gen. purpose soap 5#  . . . . . . . . . . . . . . .75
Hand soap . . . . . . . . . . . . . . . . . . . . . . . .17
Catsup . . . . . . . . . . . . . . . . . . . . . . . . . . .12
Cantaloupe  . . . . . . . . . . . . . . . . . . . . . . .06
Total . . . . . . . . . . . . . . . . . . . . . . . . . . 8.71
```

Fourth ticket:
```
SaniClor  . . . . . . . . . . . . . . . . . . . . . . . . .10
Biff . . . . . . . . . . . . . . . . . . . . . . . . . . . . . .18
5 pkg. gum . . . . . . . . . . . . . . . . . . . . . . . .25
1 doz. eggs  . . . . . . . . . . . . . . . . . . . . . . .12
Vanilla . . . . . . . . . . . . . . . . . . . . . . . . . . .43
Chore boy  . . . . . . . . . . . . . . . . . . . . . . . .09
Potatoes  . . . . . . . . . . . . . . . . . . . . . . . . .05
Pins . . . . . . . . . . . . . . . . . . . . . . . . . . . . .08
Crackers . . . . . . . . . . . . . . . . . . . . . . . . . .31
Total . . . . . . . . . . . . . . . . . . . . . . . . .  10.32
Tax . . . . . . . . . . . . . . . . . . . . . . . . . . . . .08
Grand Total . . . . . . . . . . . . . . . . . . . .  10.40
```

We bought five gallons of gas for ninety-three cents and we were ready to face the world.

The next day, Saturday the 6th, we took my younger brother and his friend frog hunting out by the river. I wasn't much interested, but the boys had a good time and they caught enough for us to have a frog legs feast for the family the next day.

That was the first time I ever tried to cook something that kept jumping around in the skillet. It was creepy! I don't think I ate very many of them.

On Sunday, we went to church, of course. Then had dinner again at my folks house.

That was our "honeymoon". We didn't know then that we wouldn't get that "real" honeymoon until we took our oldest boys away to college.

Chapter Five

RIO VISTA

We hadn't been married very long when I lost my job in Stockton. I had finished up where I had been a-workin' for the California State Highway Department. I did not get canned.

The only way that I could work was to move to where the work was and that was some forty or fifty miles away. I would still be working for the Highway Department.

Where we had to go was a little town called Rio Vista. It was where three rivers came together. They were the Mokelumne, San Joaquin, and Sacramento. That made a big wide river there.

The headquarters for the California State Highway Department was there and they repaired all of the state highways for several miles around.

Well, we decided to make the move and all that we could find to live in was an old-fashioned auto court. That is a place that has a lot of little cabins with a place on the side of each cabin to put a car. It was real small, but as long as there was not any more than just the two of us we could get by with it. About all we had was a bed in the main room and a small kitchen and a small bathroom.

This one particular day the highway crew that I was with was a-workin' in Benicia, some thirty miles away. We were repairing the highway there. The boss asked me if I wanted to be the flagman that day. That sounded like a lot of fun and not too much work, so I took it, but by ten o'clock I was a-wishin' that someone else had that job and I was working with a shovel – or anything else. I never got so tired of anything in my whole life as I did that one job. But I didn't have any choice. I had to stick it out!

It seemed like I had been there a long, long time. I didn't have a watch but it felt like it was about time to quit. And sure enough, I was given the word to let all the rest of the cars go through and then wait there till someone came to pick me up.

That sounded like a good idea to me. I was a-wantin' to go home to my new little wife and I knew that she would have supper ready when I got there.

Every truck that came down the road, I was a-hopin' that it would be the one. But it was not, and by now the sun was getting pretty low and things were getting pretty quiet. I was getting worried that they might have left me. There was no way to tell my little wife that I would be late and I knew that she would be worried by now and a-wonderin' why I was not coming home.

The highway yard was not too far from where we lived. I thought maybe she might go up there to see if my car was still there. Well, she did. In fact, she made several trips on the blue bicycle before she saw anyone.

One of the men that I worked with asked her if she was waiting for someone. She told him who she was and asked him if there were any more trucks a-comin' in.

He said, "No, that is the last one."

Then he slapped himself and said, "Oh, No! I'll bet they all went off and forgot Swannie. He was flagging at the far end of the road where we were working."

They had to send a man back to pick me up. It was already dark by the time that I got home. My poor little wife was sure happy to see me. I think that she cried for five minutes and hung on to me till she got my shirt wet with her tears.

We sat down and ate some cold fried potatoes and greens, but they tasted good to me. I was real hungry and she was a good cook.

We finished that job and the next day and we were a-workin' on one of the bridges over the San Joaquin River. We were tightening some bolts. The boss gave me a big crescent wrench to hold one of the bolts with and he had not any more than said, "Don't drop that wrench in the river," and I did. It went plum right out of my hand.

There were two fellows a-workin' with me, Archie Bollinger and Ray Pulitch. They sure gave me the razz. They were always a-kiddin' me about being a newly married man, and you never knew what they might come up with next.

One afternoon about two we could see the salmon fishing boats by the dozens with their nets a-nettin' salmon. This was quite a show. It was hard for me to tend to what I was supposed to be doing. I heard my name mentioned and when I looked around, there stood Ray with a twenty pound salmon.

He said, "Here, take this fish home with you, and me and Archie will be over for supper."

At quitting time, I took the fish and headed for home. I hadn't any more than gotten in the door, in fact, I hadn't even had a chance to kiss my little wife, when there came a knock at the door and there they were!

You see, I had been a-braggin' about what a good cook my little wife was and they were coming over to see how good she really was.

Well, I took the fish into that small kitchen and cleaned it, and as soon as I had it cut up, I went back to visit with Ray and Archie.

Pretty soon I noticed that things were awful quiet in the kitchen. Every once in a while I would look over that direction. It sounded as if my little wife was a-cryin'. The next time that I looked, she motioned for me to come into the kitchen. She was a-cryin', all right.

She said, "I have never cooked fish in my life before."

So I gave her some fast instructions and went back into the living room and sat down to continue my visit with Ray and Archie.

I want you to know that was the best fish that I ever tasted. Neither one of those guys ever knew that was the first time my sweet little wife had fried fish. That is, until some twenty years later when we happened to run across Archie Bollinger. We had a long talk about the good old times we'd had together. He still remembered the fried salmon. He thought it was the best he'd ever tasted, too.

Hubby coming home from first
day of work after marriage.

Settling Into Married Life

Chapter Six

ONE PLUS ONE EQUALS ?

That summer, (1940) the war in Europe was getting hot and heavy. Hitler and Moussilini were making their presence known in many nations nearby. The newspapers were full of war stories. Things were beginning to look very bad. The U.S. Congress passed a conscription bill that required all men age eighteen to forty-five to register for the military draft.

About two weeks after we were married, my brother, Don Robinson, joined the Army. He was just barely eighteen. He decided that rather than be drafted, he'd join the army so he could have his own choice of service.

Walter had to register along with all the other young men, but being married gave a man a little better chance of not being drafted immediately – not much, but a little.

One day we went over to the folks for dinner in the evening and we talked about the war situation and Don's joining the army. We did a lot of speculating about the situation. We were getting closer to war as each day passed. We knew it wasn't but a matter of time before the United States would be involved.

That evening, on the way to our new little home, Walter and I discussed the possibility of his being drafted. That would have been intolerable for this newly married couple who were so much in love. There seemed only one thing for us to do.

Fathers would be deferred – at least for the present time, so we decided we might just as well start our family right away. Besides, we really wanted to have a baby.

A week or two later Walter was transferred to Rio Vista where he worked for four weeks. Then he was laid off and we returned to Stockton, back to our little two room honeymoon home.

He went out looking for another job and found one right away as a laborer working for an underground construction company. By that time it was about the first of September.

Our house was about a quarter of a mile away from a big cannery and they were canning tomatoes. It was hot so I had all the windows and doors open while I was ironing Walter's work clothes.

All of a sudden the smell coming from that cannery got to me and I was sick to my stomach. I couldn't figure out why I should feel so weak and sick.

A few days later I really got sick and developed an earache and a sore throat. My ear hurt so bad I could hardly stand it. I had the flu – or something. I was very sick for about a week. My eardrum finally ruptured and I began to feel better. But even after all that I still was getting sick in the mornings.

Walter guessed before I did what was really the matter with me. I was going to have a baby!

My parents were hoping that we'd wait a little while before we had a family, so we didn't want to tell anyone right away. We tried to keep our secret, but it wasn't long till everybody knew.

Chapter Seven

MY BACK INJURY

After working in Rio Vista for four weeks I got laid off from the California Highway Department. It didn't take me long to find another job. But two weeks later I was a-headin' to the hospital in the back of an ambulance with my back a-hurtin'. I was sure that it was broken. As bad as I felt, it was bound to be. You see, I was a-workin' at this underground construction job and I fell and hurt my back.

As soon as they got me to the hospital, there were x-rays taken and it was determined that my back was not broken, although it still felt like it.

Well, they kept me there for a couple of days and told me that I could go home, that there was nothing wrong with me. But I insisted that there was. I was still a-hurtin' too bad for there not to be something wrong. I stayed there all that day till they were about ready to throw me out. Rather than make a big fuss about it, I went home.

The doctor said that I could go back to work as soon as I wanted to and felt like it. Well, I worked a half a day and my back started a-hurtin' again, so I went back to the same doctor. He didn't want to have anything to do with me, so I went to another doctor.

He was a young doctor just out of school by the name of Dr. Henry Peterson, Jr. He was very kind to me and tried to help me the best that he could with heat treatments on my back, and he told me to put a board under my mattress.

Well, I just put it on my side of the bed so that my little wife wouldn't be uncomfortable. But that didn't work very well. The bed sagged on her side and she had to sleep in a hole.

After I was off a few weeks I started to draw workmen's

compensation, which was not a whole lot, only $18.75 a week, but it was better than nothing, so I took it. But in a few weeks the insurance company stopped a-payin' me. They cut me off and there was no money a-comin' in at all. I had a pregnant wife and I was not able to work on account of my back injury and the doctor wouldn't give me a release to go back to work. I was desperate. I didn't know what to do.

I went to the Industrial Commissioner and found out that the compensation insurance company wouldn't pay because they said my problem was from the back injury I'd had seven months earlier in February while working for another construction company and it was their place to pay the compensation.

The Industrial Commissioner ordered one of the insurance companies to pay me, but I don't remember which one it was. They paid for a little while, then I was cut off again. Now it was a fight between the two workmen's compensation companies.

What happened later is told in another chapter because it happened several months later.

Chapter Eight

OUR FIRST CHRISTMAS

I hadn't been a-working for a long time because of my back injury and this made me feel real bad that I couldn't get a present for my little pregnant wife and sweetheart. I thought of every scheme that was possible and still came up with nothing. We were a-goin' over to Mom and Dad Robinson's for supper every day and getting by on whatever we could scrape up for the other two meals.

Well, one evening as we were coming home from Mom and Dad's, I looked at that old car that I had before we were married that was a-sittin' out in back. I hadn't paid very much for it in the first place and I figured that it was not worth anything at all. Maybe, I could give it to someone for the hauling off. Maybe I would even have to give them a couple of bucks to boot.

Naw, that wasn't any good either, but there had to be some way I could get the money to get a present. Even five dollars would be good. But it still stayed in my mind. This car ought to be worth something – maybe five bucks.

There was a junk yard just across the tracks on Waterloo Road not too far from where we lived. So one day I went over there just to see if I could get something out of it. Anything would be good. So I went up to the boss of the yard and started a-talking.

This is how it went.

I said, "I have a big problem. I have a little wife at home that is pregnant and I am broke and it is not long before Christmas. This is the first Christmas we have been together since we were married. I have this old car at home that don't run and all it is a pile of junk and I would like to know if it is worth anything at all.

"I don't live very far from here, just a little over a couple of blocks. Would you come over and look at it and see if you could give me anything for it at all."

He said, "Sure. I can go over right now and take a look at it."

So he hopped in his pick-up and followed me back home. We both went out and looked at it. I was ashamed of it 'cause it looked like it had gotten sunburnt and was a-peelin' the paint. The underneath coat was a different color.

He took one walk around it and started back for the pick-up and got in and I was sure that he was not going to give me anything for it at all. He did not even look at it long enough to make any kind of a decision.

Well, he started up the pick-up and as he started to drive off he said, "I will be over and get it in a little bit. I'll give you fifteen dollars for it. How is that?"

I was delighted, but there was a sound of charity in his voice. That was as much as I had paid for it a year ago, lacking three dollars.

He was not gone too long till here he came back with a wrecker, gave me fifteen dollars, and hauled it away.

Now I had enough to get the present that I wanted and I was happy about that, but my plans were all shot to pieces, 'cause Deloris woke up from her nap just as he was a-drivin' out of the driveway. She asked me who that was and I had to tell her and give her half of the money so that she could buy me a present too.

Now, that was a long time ago, but I can still remember the love that we shared with each other and how wonderful it was. I have forgotten now what it was that I got for her.

Maybe Walter has forgotten what he bought with his half of the fifteen dollars, but I haven't. We took that money, him with his half and me with my half, and went to town to spend it, joyously happy that we had enough money to buy each other a Christmas present.

He bought me a wooden nut bowl with a stob in the center to crack the nuts on and a wooden mallet to crack them with. He also bought a Sunset Magazine Cookbook. After fifty three years I still have the cookbook, although it is tattered and torn from being well used.

The only thing I could think of to buy for Walter was a pair of slippers. I walked from one end of the Main Street business section of down town Stockton, stopping in every shoe store looking for a pair of slippers big enough for him. Most stores don't carry slippers over size eleven and he need at least a twelve.

Fifty-three years later, I'm not sure whether I found them or not, but I must have because we were happy that we had managed to buy Christmas presents for each other due to Walter's resourcefulness.

Then we needed to buy presents for the family because they expected us to be with them for Christmas. Good old Henry came to the rescue. He was still working at the Stockton Co-op and he helped us. He bought a box of oranges for us to give to the family. We would pay him back later.

When we opened presents with the family, we saved our gift to the last, then Walter went out to the car and brought in our box of oranges for all of them.

They thought that was a pretty clever idea. Later we enjoyed a scrumptious turkey dinner with all the trimmings, and an orange or two (or three).

What had looked like a very unhappy event a week or two before, turned out to be a very happy and memorable occasion.

My Handsome Hubby

One Very Proud Father

Chapter Nine

ME 'N MAMA HAD TWIN BOYS

I had gone to see Dr. Peterson when I was so sick with an ear infection soon after we were married. About two months later I went to see him again and he confirmed the fact that I was going to have a baby and said that it should be due around May 15th. His fee would be seventy-five dollars for prenatal care and delivery. Walter wasn't working because of his back injury, but we thought we could pay him a little each month and that was all right with the doctor.

Then, when I was about five months along, we decided that I should go out to the county hospital because of the problems we were having with getting Walter's compensation. So I went there for my prenatal care.

A Dr. Hansen examined me and said that I was seven months pregnant. I was indignant about that deduction.

I said, "I can't be. I've only been married five months."

"Well," he said, "Sometimes that doesn't make any difference. You're either at seven months or you're having twins."

I liked the "having twins" idea better. From the time that I was ten years old I had said that someday I was going to have twins.

I was getting big fast and the neighbors and friends were counting on their fingers. That didn't bother us. I guess I had a right to be big. Before it was over there was eleven pounds of baby in there. We were excited about the possibility of having twins and the closer the delivery date came the more sure we were that we would be having twins.

At six months my little wife was not so little any more. She waddled like a duck when she walked and was twice as big as I thought she ought to be.

One morning, about six or seven weeks before the baby was due, she woke up with a stomach ache. We'd gone out to have some chow mein the evening before and bought some doughnuts afterwards. She thought her stomach ache was from the food she'd eaten. It was too soon for the baby to come by more than six weeks. Since this was her first baby, she didn't realize what kind of pains she was having.

We went over to her folks house and she laid around all day, sometimes hurting and sometimes feeling pretty good. But towards evening, her mother went into the living room where I was a-sitting. She knew what was going on!

She had a real mad look on her face as she said to me, "You'd better call that doctor right now!"

I said, "OK, **OK**! I will!"

We had just received a pretty good sized payment from the compensation insurance company after they had been ordered to do it and I had some money to pay him. So I called Dr. Peterson and he came out to the house and examined Deloris.

All of the time he was there her mother was worried, and as soon as the doctor came out of the bedroom she asked him what was the matter with her.

All he said as he walked out the door was, "She is getting ready to have a baby, maybe two of them. If her pains get harder take her to the hospital and call me. If not we'll take x-rays tomorrow."

Now this put all together a different expression on her face, as she said, "If Deloris is going to have that baby tonight I'd better go get her a nightgown to wear at the hospital." And she left for the store.

Before Mom could get back, Dad and I decided that maybe we'd better get Deloris to the hospital right away. So we bundled her up in her old bathrobe, put her in our car, and headed for the hospital. I remember it was about 10:00 p.m. when we left to take her to Dameron Hospital.

In those days the dads all had to sit in the waiting room and wait for the good word. While I was a-waitin', there was another man waiting for word from his wife. She had gone in just a little ahead of Deloris by about twenty minutes. We were a-sittin' there visiting. He was telling me that he had three girls and this time it was going to be a boy. He knew because boys are usually bigger than girls and his wife was definitely bigger this time.

Just about that time we heard a baby cry. He smiled and said, "That is yours. It sounds like a girl."

I said, "Nope. That is not mine. I will know when my baby cries." And very shortly, another baby cried.

He said, "That's yours this time."

And I said, "Nope. That is not mine, either. It is yours."

We waited for several minutes more. Then there was a little squeak of a baby cry.

I said, "That is mine." About ten minutes later there was another cry.

Then he said, "I suppose that one is yours, too."

And I said, "Yep, that is mine."

Then, pretty soon, here came the nurse.

She said, "Mr. Swan, your wife has presented you with a fine set of boys."

Then she turned to the other fellow and said, "Your wife has presented you with a fine set of girls."

All he said was, "That is great! Five girls! That is **just** great!"

There were four sets of twins born that weekend in that hospital, the only time in the history of the city of Stockton that that has ever happened. It was Palm Sunday, the 6th of April 1941.

Our baby boys were born at 12:44 and 12:54 a.m. They weighed five pounds even and six pounds even. We had planned to name our first boy child James Albert after his father and paternal grandfather. When the office girl brought the papers I needed to fill out for their names I put down James Albert for the six pound baby and Gerald Ray (Ray is my father's name) for the five pound baby. We'd call them Jimmy and Jerry.

On the ninth day after their birth, the office girl brought me the hospital birth certificates with their footprints on them. They had number one twin on Jerry's certificate and number two twin on Jimmy's certificate. I told her that was wrong. The first baby was supposed to be James Albert. She told me then, that the first baby was the five pound one, not the six pound one! I don't know why I thought that the six pound baby was born first.

When Walter came in to see me I was crying.

I said, "Oh, Honey, what are we going to do? I've named the babies wrong." And I sobbed on his shoulder.

"Never mind, Mama," he said, "Don't cry. It's all right that way." And so Jimmy and Jerry got each others names, and that's the way we always said their names, never Jerry and Jimmy. From then on we called each other Daddy and Mama, except for the times we say Honey or Sweetheart.

In those days new mamas had to stay in the hospital ten days. My hospital bill was sixty dollars for the ten days with one dollar extra a day for the extra baby. We just barely had enough money to pay the hospital.

We had to leave the babies in the hospital for a few more days because of their premature birth. Two or three days later we went to get Jimmy, the bigger twin.

We had noticed on his birth certificate footprint that it showed only four toes on his right foot. We thought they had just missed one.

When I dressed him to bring him home I looked at his toes. Sure enough there were only four toes on his right foot and that leg was just a bit shorter than the left one. (That has been a problem to him all of his life, but more about that later.)

As a teenager I never had the opportunity to babysit except for two or three times for the neighbor across the street. I didn't take any classes in my schooling that would prepare me for motherhood, either, but when I picked up Jimmy and held him in my arms to take him home, all my natural mothering instincts flowered at once. I <u>knew</u> what I needed to do for my babies.

Jerry had to stay there a few more days. I guess it was a good thing because it gave me a little chance to get used to taking care of a baby before I had the two of them. Daddy still wasn't working because of his back injury so he was a VERY BIG help to me. He would get up in the middle of the night when they cried, change them, and bring them to me to nurse.

Shortly after we got home from the hospital a neighbor came over to see the babies. I was nursing one of them – which I seemed to be doing all of the time.

He said, "You've got two nose bags. Why don't you feed them both at the same time?"

After he left, Daddy said, "Let's try it!" So he propped up a pillow on each side of me as I laid on the bed and laid a baby on each side. And it worked! For six months I nursed both of them that way.

When we took the babies and me to the doctor for our six-weeks check up, we parked the car more than two blocks away from the doctor's office. After we were done there, we left the office with Daddy carrying one baby and me carrying the other.

We were so proud of our twins that we didn't want to just walk back to the car. We walked two blocks up to Main Street, turned and walked two blocks towards the direction of our car, then walked back the two blocks to our car. We went six blocks out of our way to get there. We were well rewarded for our efforts. Everyone stared and "Oh-ed" and "Ah-ed". And we busted our buttons off!

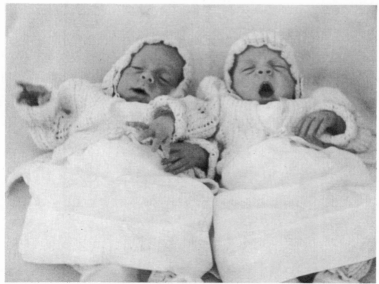

Jerry and Jimmy at six weeks

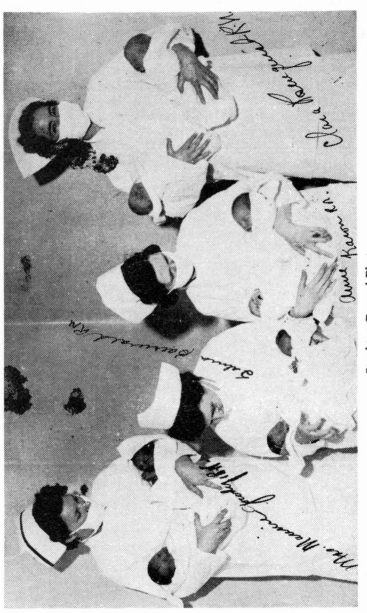

Stockton Record Photo

Proud Mama

Grandpa and Grandma with the twins

"me 'n Mama"

Mama and our twins, Jimmy and Jerry

Chapter Ten

THE BIRTHDAY CAKE

It was getting pretty close to my twentieth birthday. The two insurance companies were still haggling over which one was to pay Daddy's compensation. Of course, he wasn't working, yet. We were in a financial bind. Daddy was worrying about where he was going to get the money to buy me something for my birthday. I told him not to worry. If we didn't have it, we didn't have it.

Mom said that she would give me the money for a permanent for my birthday. Daddy said he'd take care of the babies for me while I went to the beauty shop. That was enough birthday present from him. So I made my appointment and went to get the permanent on my birthday.

It seemed like it was taking an awfully long time and I began to worry about my babies being hungry. They wouldn't take a bottle because they were used to nursing.

When I got home, the babies were crying and I felt so guilty for leaving them for so long that I cried, too. They settled down just as soon as they were snuggled up to nurse.

Then Daddy brought out a birthday cake and presented it to me. I was very surprised. He had made it and decorated it all by himself, even with colored frosting! I was so delighted with it that I wouldn't cut it until we had taken a picture of it.

This was a small act of kindness, but it was a big thing to me. It was just such caring acts as this that has kept our love growing.

The Birthday Cake

Chapter Eleven

CARROLL AVENUE

The twins, Jimmy and Jerry, were getting bigger all of the time and we had already started a-lookin' for a place to rent that was a little bigger and that had a back yard where the twins could play.

One afternoon we were over at their grandparents, Mom and Dad Robinson. We were a-talkin' about getting a bigger place to live. Mom said that she would take care of the boys if we wanted to go look for a place. That sounded like a good idea so we took her up on it.

We got in the Model A Ford and started a-looking around. We wanted a place that was close to the folks so the twins could see their grandma and grandpa often.

I looked over at Mama and said, "Where shall we start?"

She said, "Oh, anywhere is as good as the next."

So we went just two streets down from Sinclair St. where the folks lived and started up North Carroll Ave. a-lookin'. We soon came across a place on the left that had a for sale sign on it.

I stopped the car and said, "I'll go talk to them and see if they will rent it to us."

It was a cute little white house on half an acre with a hedge all around it. It had a nice front lawn.

It was just perfect and just what we wanted. So I went up and knocked on the door. A lady answered and invited us in and we started to talk.

She was a-tellin' us what a good house it was and that the place had a well on it and you could raise all of the garden that you wanted. It even had a cool room in the back that you could store canned foods in.

She went on and on and finally she said, "The only thing it does not have is a bathroom." And after a while she ran down a little.

I asked her if she would rent it to us and she said no, that she wanted to sell it 'cause her husband was a-workin' over on the coast. She was just staying there long enough to sell the house, then she would go and join him.

We asked her what she wanted for it and she said that she wanted eighteen hundred dollars for it. She wanted three hundred fifty dollars down and fifteen dollars a month with three percent interest till it was paid for.

I thought that this was a real bargain and I said, "We will take it. We'll be back."

When we were in the car Mama looked over at me and said, "We don't have three dollars much less three hundred and fifty dollars."

"I will borrow it," I answered.

She said, "Well, all right, but how are you going to do that?"

"I don't know, but this sure is a pretty place isn't it?"

"It sure is. I would like to have it."

"Well, let's see if Dad can help us a little."

As soon as we walked into the folks house, Mom said, "You guys weren't gone very long. Did you find a house to rent this soon?"

I said, "No, but we found one that we could buy. That is, if we could get a little help from Dad."

He asked, "What kind of help are you talking about?"

"Well, we found this dandy little place just over two streets from here. They only want three hundred and fifty dollars down and fifteen dollars a month with only three percent interest. Why don't you and Mom come with us and look at it?"

So we bundled up the babies and all went over and took another look at it. It really impressed Dad.

As soon as we got back to the folks house Dad said, "That is a real good buy. I'll go down to the bank in the morning with you Walter and co-sign for you so you can get the money and you can pay it off as soon as you get back to work."

Mama and I were so happy that it brought tears to our eyes. Could this be possible that we could have our own little house?

Well, we had no problem a-gettin' the money and we went over there and took it to the woman right away. We had the papers all signed and we could move in in a couple of days. That was almost as happy of a day as the day we were married.

It didn't take us long to move what little we had with Dad's help. Then I went back for the final load by myself. I was a-drivin' up Main Street when I heard an awful noise. I looked back and saw our chamber pot that we used at night so we wouldn't have to go out to the outhouse, a-rollin' down the middle of the street. Cars were a-goin' around it and you could see the people who had seen what happened a-laughin'. The lid went one way and the pot went the other way.

I didn't know if I should keep on a-goin' or stop and pick it up. I would have to go and buy another one if I didn't stop 'cause we needed it where we were a-movin' to, so I pulled over and stopped and went and got it. My face was red and I looked down so I couldn't see people a-laughin' at me. This time I made sure that it couldn't fall off again.

I kept this secret for a long time. I was too embarrassed to tell it then, but I don't mind sharing it with you now.

Well, it took us a week or so before we got settled in and we were sure happy to have this nice little house. All the inside walls were of knotty pine and the floors were wood. It was a real comfortable little house and it was ours. Well, almost, it would be as soon as we got it paid for. We had been paying that much for rent every month and now, when it would be paid for we'd have something more than a handful of rent receipts.

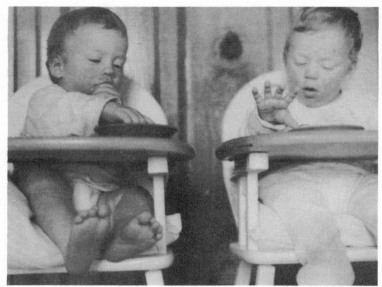

Jerry and Jimmy

Jerry and Jimmy On Carroll Avenue

Chapter Twelve

THE REST OF THE BACK INJURY STORY

By this time I had been off work for nearly nine months. We still were not getting my compensation checks the way we were supposed to. So I went to town and hired myself an attorney.

Well, he succeeded in getting a hearing with the Industrial Commission after two months. If it wasn't for my brother, Henry, I think we would have starved to death. My in-laws helped, too.

Then, suddenly, it seemed, the big day was at hand. I had to go to San Francisco for the hearing and it was just about ready to start.

The judge rapped his gavel on the table and called the court to order. He turned to my attorney and asked him to state what the issue in the case was. The attorney hemmed and hawed for about fifteen minutes. I could see that the judge was getting a little bit irritated, and so was I.

I turned to the judge and said, "Your, honor, I don't want to be disrespectful, but could I say something?"

He looked at me and said, "Yes. Go ahead."

I asked, "Is it possible to fire my attorney at this time?"

He said that I could, so I turned to my attorney and said, "You are fired!"

The judge then said to the attorney, "You are dismissed from this case. I fix your fee at twenty-five dollars."

Then the battle began. I stated the issue of the case and the hearing proceeded. There were two workmen's compensation insurance company lawyers, each representing a different company, one for each time that I had gotten hurt. They were trying to prove that it was the other one's responsibility to pay me compensation, and I was caught in the middle.

Both of them were real sharp lawyers. For a little while I felt that I was no match for the two of them. What one of them didn't think of, the other one did. The only hope that I had was to make them repeat their questions three or four times – or as many times as I thought I could get away with.

Well, the hearing lasted for about two hours and the two lawyers left. The judge told me before I left, that if I did not start getting my checks within a week to let him know.

I watched for the mailman every day. Still there was no check. I was about to give up on the whole thing when I got some encouragement from my wife. So I called the judge in San Francisco and he told me to come and see him at his office.

So I went. He talked to me for a long time and asked me what I would do if he was to get me a settlement. I said that I would pay off all of my bills and pay back my brother, Henry, for all that he had done for me and my family.

Again, he said, "If you don't get a check from the insurance company within a week let me know."

He seemed real impressed and I went home feeling good about what had happened.

I waited a full week and then I called him. That did the trick! It was not but a day or two till there was a check in the mail for $997.43 and a letter stating that I had a twenty-two and a half percent permanent disability rating. (That letter came in very handy a few years later. I'll tell you about that in another chapter.)

The first thing that I did was to pay all of my bills, including the $350.00 I had borrowed from the bank for a down payment on our little house on Carroll Ave.

What a relief it was not to have to worry with that problem any more. Now I had a new one.

I felt that it was time for me to get back to work to take care of my little family. So the first thing I did was to go see my doctor. He gave me a release. Now, at last, I could go back to work.

Jimmy and Jerry were five months old by now.

Chapter Thirteen

DRIVING BUSES FOR THE
STOCKTON CITY LINES

One day in September of 1941, one of our friends came over to see us and to see our new house. He said that where he worked they were hiring bus drivers and that I might be able to get a job there if I wanted it. So the next morning I went down to the Stockton City Lines and asked for a job.

You see, the City of Stockton had just retired all of their street cars and replaced them with buses. With so many young men being drafted they were having a hard time getting enough drivers, so I got the job.

At first I worked the extra board and worked just part of the time, but it was not long till I was a-workin' on a regular basis. This was quite an experience for me. One real foggy morning I was a-runnin a little late. Oh, I guess it was somewhere around eight when I was a-goin' north on California Street, trying my best to make up a little time so the people that were a-goin' to work would not be late on my account.

All of a sudden a car coming from my right was in a hurry, too, and ran into the side of the bus. Or, I should say, it hit the rear wheels and spun around. There was no one hurt and so I got in the bus and continued on my way. It looked like there wasn't too much damage.

Well, someone called in to the boss and told him that one of the buses had a wreck and gave him my bus number. The next trip up California Street, when I passed in front of the bus barn, the boss waved me in to the barn and put another bus on my route.

For a while I thought I would be a-lookin' for another job. He was furious at the way I had handled the situation.

Well, after he had run down a bit and I could say something, I said that I was sorry, but I had never received any instructions as to what to do in case of a problem such as this.

Now things started a-lookin' a little better for me. I spent the rest of the day filling out reports and receiving instructions. I guess that was a good lesson. I never did that again. But I did do some other things.

The next thing that happened to me was when I was running a little late – again. I was getting all of my passengers, plus those for the bus that followed me. It was one of those kinds of a situation that, when you got behind, there was no way that you could catch up, at all. So I figured out if I was to take a short cut through town and get back on time it would be a smart thing to do. So that was what I did. I was on time once again, but the phone started to ring off the wall in the office 'cause all of the passengers that I had left a-waitin' on the street corner were all late for work. My boss was told about it and as soon as I came into the bus barn after the shift, I was reminded that it was not such a smart thing to do and I almost got fired again. I did not do that stunt again.

I began to learn to run just a little ahead of time by a minute or so. Then there was not quite as many passengers 'cause most people get to the bus stop right on time and I would have been gone and they would have had to wait for the next bus.

One time I was a-goin' north on California Street. Everything was a-goin' just fine. I was on time and the weather was good. It was about ten in the morning and the bus was about half full when I was making a left turn on to Pine Street, all of a sudden I heard the most gosh awful sound and I felt my bus jerk a little. I caught a quick glance in the rear view mirror to see if I could find out what had happened.

There, right in the middle of the street, was a motorcycle flopped over on its side, its wheels a-goin' ninety miles an hour, with a cop under it. He was scared to move 'cause he was afraid of getting caught in the wheel spokes of that motorcycle that was still a-goin'. I got out of the bus and ran to him. The first thing that I did was go and shut off the motor and as soon as it stopped, I pulled him out from under it. I didn't see any blood so I figured that he was not hurt too much. But one thing that I did notice was the color of his BVDs 'cause his motorcycle britches were ripped in the crotch from the inside of the knee to the other one and he was having an awful time of keeping himself decent.

The only way he could do that was to lay down on the street and gather up the part of his britches that were ripped with both hands. He seemed real mad at me for something or another.

As soon as I saw that he was all right, I went back to my bus and as I was a-duckin' my head to get into the bus I said, "Even cops make mistakes," and I started a-lookin around for the accident cards that I was to give to all of the passengers on the bus. I asked them to fill the cards out and to tell what they had seen happen and who's fault it was.

I hadn't gotten them all passed out when I could hear sirens a-comin' from every direction. In a matter of minutes that street was a-swarmin' with cops and here came an ambulance, too. Then here came an over fed, city police officer. How I knew that was 'cause he had a lot of stripes on the sleeve of his shirt.

He said, "Come on, you're going with me."

I said, "I'm sorry officer, but I can't go right now. I have to collect up all of these accident cards from the passengers first. Then I have to make out an accident report. As soon as I get that all done, I'll do anything that you want me to do."

I remembered the instructions from the last time that I had a wreck with the bus. I knew what would happen to me if I didn't get those reports. I'd be sure to get fired.

By then, they had loaded the motorcycle cop into the ambulance and they were leaving with their siren going full blast.

I gathered up all of the cards and was a-makin' out my report as best I could with this impatient officer a-waiting for me to hurry up and finish.

Upon checking all of the cards, everyone of them said that it was the cop's fault. One of them even said that the cop had ought to have known better 'cause we always turn on Pine Street and he was just plain not watching where he was a-goin'.

I handed all of the cards to the officer so that he could make out his report. He thumbed through them and went to the back of the bus and talked to the passengers about what had happened. By then he had cooled off a little and when he was through, he let me go to finish up my run.

But before I could get the bus started, here came my boss a-drivin'up in a company car. He wasted no time getting out and coming over to the bus. He started yelling at me a-makin' the air blue. He was so excited that I had a hard time of understanding him. Then he talked to the officer for a while. Then everything was all okay and I was on my way.

When I got in that evening, I was complimented by the boss on the good job that I did handling the situation.

There was a couple of other young men a-drivin' buses as well as me, but the rest of them were older men. I mean, like in their fifties or sixties. Being one of the young men, sometimes this turned out to be a problem for me.

I was always friendly with all of the passengers that got on the bus and sometimes some of the young women would mistake my friendliness to mean something else.

One day a young lady brought me a nice batch of cookies. I thanked her for them and told her that was mighty nice of her, that I would take them home and share them with my wife and twin boys. She had a disappointed expression on her face.

I loved my wife and I didn't want this young woman to get any funny ideas. I didn't know it at the time, but there were several of them who had their eyes on me.

There was this particular time that I had the night run from East Main Street to the college which took an hour to make. The shift ended at midnight. There was this young lady who got on the bus away out on East Main Street. She was still on when I came to the end of the run.

I told her that this was the end of the line and asked her if she missed getting off at the right place. She started to talk to me saying that she had a date with her boy friend and he had stood her up, that she was bored and wanted something to do. She wanted to know if she could ride around with me for a while. I felt sorry for her and said that she could.

Well, she sat in the seat just behind me and talked all of the time. It was a-gettin' late and I told her that I just had one more trip to make and that she had better make up her mind about where she wanted to get off 'cause I was heading for the bus barn and I was going home after that. She said that she'd get off there.

Then she tried to get me to take her out for a cup of coffee on my way home. When I turned her down, she wanted me to just park the bus for a couple of minutes and talk. By then, it was clear to me what she was after and I tried to get her to get off the bus some place. I didn't care where and I told her again that I was going to the barn. Maybe there was somebody there that would buy her a cup of coffee and that is just what happened.

I told one of the bus drivers that there was a young woman in my bus that wanted someone to buy her a cup of coffee and take her home. Well, this bus driver jumped at the chance and he took her home.

I heard sometime later that was the wrong thing for him to do. That act caused him a lot of misery. He and his wife separated over that incident.

Well, this kind of a situation was not getting any better as time went on. I didn't like hurting people's feelings, but I didn't know what to do about it. I talked it over with Mama and we decided to change jobs.

I heard that the railroad needed help and were a-hirin' at this time. Everybody that applied for a job, got it. So I told my boss that I was quitting. He didn't like it very much. He had put up with all of my blunders for a long time and I was just beginning to be a good bus driver and now I was quitting.

But me 'n Mama and our babies were more important than driving a bus for other people. Besides, the railroad paid a lot better than bus driving.

Walter on his last day of driving buses.
June 26, 1942

Chapter Fourteen

LUCILLE

We had been in our new home on Carroll Avenue only a few days when our next door neighbor came over to get acquainted and visit for a little while. She was the same age as Daddy. Her husband, Del, worked for the Santa Fe Railroad. He was a section foreman, building and repairing the railroad tracks for the Santa Fe Railroad. They had two little boys, Delbert and Bobby, ages four and two.

Lucille had a very "salty" tongue, but she was fun to be with and to visit with. She was also a very compassionate person. I think she began to feel sorry for me because I was having to take care of two babies. She could see that it was a lot of work.

One day she came over when I was nursing the babies in the bedroom. My closet door was open and she could see a lot of clothes piled up in one corner of it.

She asked, "What in the *@^# are all of those clothes doing piled up in your closet?"

"Well," I answered, "That's my ironing that I haven't done, yet." I didn't tell her that I didn't like to iron, so I just ironed what I needed when I needed it. The next day Lucille came over with her iron and ironing board.

"Okay, girl!" she said, "Get out your ironing board and let's clean up this ^#@* mess!"

Lucille was a lot taller than I am (and a lot louder, too) I didn't think I'd better say no to her, and we spent the rest of the day getting my ironing caught up.

She is the only neighbor who ever did that for me. She was always helping with one thing or another.

We hadn't been living on Carroll Avenue very long before Walter found a pig to buy. It was a large sow and she was going to have little pigs soon.

55

One day before Daddy left for work, he told me to make sure to keep an eye on the sow. When I went to check on her I could see that she was starting to have her babies.

Lucille came over and we played midwives to that big old sow. I think she had six or seven little pigs. By the time she was done she was shaking and shivering. Lucille went home and found an old blanket and we covered the sow with it. We were afraid she was going to die and we didn't know what else to do for her. When our husbands got home they had a big laugh over the blanket on the pig, but we got praise for doing a good job with her.

When Daddy got hurt in the shipyard, (you'll hear about that later), Lucille did a lot of baby sitting for me while Daddy was in the hospital. She insisted that I use her car when he was ready to come home. She was afraid that our old Model A Ford would be too rough riding for him.

Later on, Lucille's husband, Del, got drafted into the Army with a captain's rank. The government desperately needed people with his skills to build and repair railroads overseas. So Lucille and Del sold their house thinking that he'd be getting his orders within thirty days, the amount of time they would have to get out of their house. Lucille was planning to take their boys and move to Kansas to live with her mother for the duration of the war.

Well, when the thirty days were up, Del still hadn't received his orders. They had to get out of their house and had no place to go, so we invited them to come and stay with us until he left.

It was a little crowded, but we all managed to get by for the few weeks they were with us. When Del reported for duty in the Army, Lucille left with the two boys. We didn't see them again until after the war was over. Then they returned to our part of the country and Del was working for the Santa Fe Railroad again.

We renewed our acquaintance with them and they have been good family friends ever since.

P.S. Lucille's tongue is no longer "salty".

Chapter Fifteen

THE BEGINNING OF THE WAR YEARS

It was after Thanksgiving and a week into December. We decided to take the babies and go out to the country to the turkey farm to buy a turkey for Christmas. There was a farmer out in French Camp who had a good buy on them, live. (This was before the days of frozen turkeys in the supermarket.)

It was quite early in the day when we got there. Someone had his radio on just as loud as he could get it. Every one there was standing around close to it. They were listening with sad faces and tears. They were getting the news that the Japanese had bombed Pearl Harbor, Hawaii. World War II had begun for the United States!

Jimmy and Jerry were just eight months old. Daddy was still driving the buses for the City Lines. Nobody knew what effect the coming war years would have on them and their families. We didn't know, then, that it would be four and a half years before it would be over. It was the morning of December 7, 1941.

We were among the fortunate who never suffered the loss of a close loved one. During the war there were plenty of jobs for those who wanted to work. So for us it was a time of relative prosperity after the struggle that we had been through with Daddy's back injury.

We listened to the news every day which made us feel sorry that such things were going on, but it didn't affect us personally, too much.

It wasn't long until the U.S. Government put food, gasoline, tires, and clothing on ration. Each person was given a ration stamp book, including the babies. Nearly everything we bought not only cost us money, but also ration stamps.

Jimmy and Jerry didn't require too many stamps to feed and clothe them, so we had plenty for ourselves. It didn't matter which book the stamps came from. If you worked in a war industry or ran a farm, you got a few extra gasoline stamps. So we never ran short of stamps for what we needed.

UNITED STATES OF AMERICA
OFFICE OF PRICE ADMINISTRATION

607071 EH

WAR RATION BOOK No. 3 *Void if altered*

Identification of person to whom issued: PRINT IN FULL

_James___ A._____ Swan_____
(First name) (Middle name) (Last name)

Street number or rural route _203 S. Carroll_

City or post office _Stockton_ State _Calif._

AGE	SEX	WEIGHT	HEIGHT	OCCUPATION
2	m	37 Lbs.	3 Ft. 1 In.	

SIGNATURE _James A. Swan_ (mother)
(Person to whom book is issued. If such person is unable to sign because of age or incapacity, another may sign in his behalf.)

WARNING
This book is the property of the United States Government. It is unlawful to sell it to any other person, or to use it or permit anyone else to use it, except to obtain rationed goods in accordance with regulations of the Office of Price Administration. Any person who finds a lost War Ration Book must return it to the War Price and Rationing Board which issued it. Persons who violate rationing regulations are subject to $10,000 fine or imprisonment, or both.

OPA Form No. R-130

LOCAL BOARD ACTION

Issued by _____
(Local board number) (Date)

Street address _____

City _____ State _____

BOOK 4

(Signature of issuing officer)

NOT VALID WITHOUT STAMP

RATION STAMP NO. 1	RATION STAMP NO. 2	RATION STAMP NO. 3	RATION STAMP NO. 4
RATION STAMP NO. 5	RATION STAMP NO. 6	RATION STAMP NO. 7	RATION STAMP NO. 8
RATION STAMP NO. 9	RATION STAMP NO. 10	RATION STAMP NO. 11	RATION STAMP NO. 12
RATION STAMP NO. 13	RATION STAMP NO. 14	RATION STAMP NO. 15	RATION STAMP NO. 16
RATION STAMP NO. 17	RATION STAMP NO. 18	RATION STAMP NO. 19	RATION STAMP NO. 20
RATION STAMP NO. 21	RATION STAMP NO. 22	RATION STAMP NO. 23	RATION STAMP NO. 24
RATION STAMP NO. 25	RATION STAMP NO. 26	RATION STAMP NO. 27	RATION STAMP NO. 28

World War II Ration Book and Stamps

You couldn't buy a new car because they weren't making any. The automobile manufacturing industries were making war machinery. We couldn't have afforded one, anyway.

Not too long after we were married, one of my uncles died and my parents inherited his 1936 Plymouth sedan. So we inherited the old Model A Ford from my parents. While my parents owned it, it was named Penelope, and that was what we called it as long as we had it. Penelope served us well and lasted as long as we needed her.

I think we "suffered" from not being able to buy rubber pants for the babies as much as anything else. I spent a lot of time knitting "soakers" with wool yarn. They weren't the best "wetness protectors" but they were far better than nothing. Life, for us went on just about the same.

On the day that Jimmy and Jerry had their first birthday, I dressed up in my wedding dress and dressed the boys in their best "bib and tucker", then met Daddy in town. We went to the photo studio and had our first real family photo taken. You can see the results in the following pictures.

Jimmy and Jerry on Their First Birthday
April 6, 1942

Deloris holding Jimmy   Walter holding Jerry

Chapter Sixteen

DADDY'S LITTLE HELPERS

The house we had bought on Carroll Avenue was a-gettin' a little small and there was a need for more room. We did not have a bathroom, so we decided to add on bedroom, a bath, and a sun porch.

I tore down a tank house for one of the local farmers for the lumber. It was real good lumber – redwood siding and rough-sawed two by fours, and some two by sixes in it, too. This took a long time 'cause I was very careful not to split up the boards any more than necessary. Even at that, we had to buy some lumber and other stuff. So we took out a loan to get the plumbing and the roof. It was a lot of fun a-puttin' it together.

The rest of the house was all knotty pine on the inside and was very beautiful and we wanted to keep it all a-lookin' the same. The plumbing is what I had the most trouble with, but I got my father-in-law to help me with that.

The rainy season was fast approaching and I was a-workin' on the roof, putting on wood shingles. I was all but finished. In fact, I was putting the cap on one day when I looked in back of me and there was Jimmy and Jerry, our nineteen-month-old twins. They had both climbed up on that roof and were a-wantin' to help me. I was scared to death that they might loose their balance and fall off. So I eased over and got a hold of both of them and called for their mother.

I guess she didn't hear me 'cause the radio was a-goin' in the house. So I just sat there with one in each arm on the peek of the roof a-waitin' till she came out of the house with another load of clothes to hang on the line – and that seemed like it was forever.

When she saw that I had both of the boys up on the roof, she said, "What in the world are you doing with both of those boys up there? Don't you know that they might fall off there? What is the matter with you, anyway, Daddy?" She was really giving me heck!

As soon as she run down a little, I told her that they had climbed the ladder all by themselves and for her to climb the ladder and take one of them from me and I would take the other one down. Well, we got the boys down and nobody got hurt. After that, whenever I was on the roof, Mama made sure she knew where the babies were.

It was about that same time that I had bought a hundred baby chicks and I had noticed that they were disappearing till there were just a few of them left. So I started a-lookin' around to find out what happened to them. I discovered that the neighbor next door to us had a big black cat and it was eating them as fast as she got hungry. I saw her a-sittin' in the neighbor's back yard and it was an easy shot with the twenty-two rifle to pick her off. I went into the house and got the rifle and went outside to shoot that cat.

I was about to pull the trigger when from behind me, Mama was screaming at the top of her voice, "**DADDY! PLEASE DON'T!**"

So I put the gun down and as I did I noticed a cardboard box just the other side of this cat and a little boy was crawling out of it from where he had been a-playin' in it. If Mama had not stopped me, I could have hit that little boy! I was so very grateful to her for that. That taught me a lesson. Never shoot where you can't see and don't let your mad get the best of you.

Somewhere along about this time we decided to take the twins to see their Grandpa Swan who lived in Bisbee, Arizona. Daddy was in between jobs and we thought this would be a good time to go.

We put our suitcases on the floor in front of the back seat of the old Model A Ford sedan and filled in the empty spaces with boxes or pillows, then put the baby crib mattress over the seat and boxes to make a sleeping and playing place for the babies. And we made that trip to Arizona.

Grandpa Swan was pleased as punch to see the boys and they had a grand time playing together. It rained while we were there and Jimmy and Jerry left muddy hand prints on Grandpa's front door. He would never let anyone wash them off.

Everything went well driving back until we got about a hundred miles from home. We should have stopped at a motel and rested, but we were anxious to get home. We were running a little short of cash, anyway. You always figure you can make it another one hundred miles. The babies were sleeping so peacefully that we didn't want to disturb them. So we continued driving. We both got so sleepy that we would have to take fifteen minute to thirty minute turns so we could keep going.

We finally arrived home about 1:00 a.m. When we took the boys out of the car to take them into the house, they woke up and became frightened. I think they must have wakened the whole neighborhood with their crying.

Lucille came over early the next morning and asked, "What in the #@^* were you doing to those kids last night?"

Well, at least the neighbors knew we were home and we were one happy family to be home again.

Jimmy and Jerry at Grandpa Swan's

Daddy's Little Helpers

Daddy's Little Helpers
working on the Model A Ford

Chapter Seventeen

WORKING ON THE RAILROAD

It was in the early summer of 1942 that I walked into the railroad yard of the Western Pacific fully outfitted to go to work as a brakeman. There were butterflies in my stomach and I was afraid that someone might make some wise crack and I wouldn't know what to say.

I walked into the yard office and looked on the board and saw that I was scheduled to go to the northern part of the state. Beeber was the name of the little town that I was to go to.

I was somewhat confused, so I asked the yard master what it all meant. He said that I was to take a tour of the Western Pacific Railroad system and get acquainted with all of the places and to learn about the duties of a brakeman.

I was given a little book that had all of the railroad rules in it and I was supposed to know what they all meant within thirty days. I was reading that rule book whenever I had a chance. I wanted to know as much as I could, as fast as I could.

I was introduced to the head brakeman and we climbed aboard the big Malley steam engine headed for Sacramento, California. It was a real thrill to be a part of such power and feel the clickity-click under my feet. When the engineer blew the whistle, it meant that we were on our way. Nobody called an engineer by that name. Some one told me that they called the engine a "hog", so the engineer was always the "hog head".

I soon found out that there was a strong rivalry between the engine crew and the train crew. I guess it was because we told the hog head what to do. When we got to Sacramento, I was left at the head end with the fireman and the hog head while the conductor and the brakeman went to the caboose to get a cup of coffee. They gave me to understand that I was to ride the head end to the next stop.

As we were a-pullin' out of town and weren't up to speed yet, I saw a red flag in the middle of the track propped up with some rocks. I called it to the attention of the hog head. I could tell that he was irritated when he said that it was nothing.

I said, "It might be and I think we had better stop."

This made him mad, but he stopped, anyway, and he told me to get out to see what was the reason for the flag being there. I looked and looked, but it looked all right to me, and I started to get back on so we could go. Out of the corner of my eye, I saw a figure get into one of the gondolas. I told the hog head what I saw and he held up the train till I could go see what it was.

The first gondola I looked in, there was a bum over in the corner. He offered me a cigar if I would not put him off.

"That's okay," I said, "Keep your cigar. I don't smoke, anyway. I'm a-lookin' for someone that got on. Do you know where he is? It looked like a little kid."

He motioned to the other end of the gondola, so I went over there. There, under a piece of paper, was a little boy. I don't think he was much over seven or eight, at the most. He had half a loaf of bread with the end of the wrapper all twisted up. He had a scared look on his face. I guess he knew he was in trouble.

I asked him where he was a-goin' and he said that he was running away from home and was a-goin' to Reno, Nevada to get a job as a dishwasher in a restaurant. I talked to him a little while and told him it would be best to go back home for it got real cold at night and he didn't have a coat. Besides, he might get hurt and he wouldn't feel very good about that.

I helped him out of the gondola and watched till he was in the clear. For some reason, this really got to that hog head and his attitude was a lot better towards me after that.

It was not long till the conductor came to the head end by the way of walking on top of the train. He wanted to know what was a-happenin' up here. As soon as he found out he was well pleased that we had seen the little boy before he got hurt.

It was soon dark and there was not a whole lot to do but just ride. The end of the run found us in the tall pines and the smell was out of this world. I slept on the floor in the caboose that night.

When morning came we had a new crew and a streamline diesel engine and we could see right in front of us, not at all like the steam engines with the long front end on them. We were going up the Feather River Canyon a-headin' for Nevada.

I saw more wild life in the natural state than I ever did in my whole life before. There were deer and antelope. You name it and it was there. I thoroughly enjoyed myself and, for a time, had forgotten that I was supposed to be a-workin' on that train.

The next stop was Kedde. It was a railroad stop and that was all. Not much of a town there, just a restaurant and a lodge for the trout fishermen. And a few slot machines. We had crossed the state line and were in Nevada.

There was a man who had just put two dollars in dimes in one of the slot machines. He walked away in disgust. I reached in my pocket and felt a dime there. I pulled it out and put it in the same machine and pulled the handle not really expecting anything to happen.

All of a sudden, here came dimes a-pourin' out until there was half a hat full! I gathered them up and put in another dime to clear the machine. And it did it again!

This time a man came a-runnin' over to where I was and said, "That thing is out of order!" And he gathered up all of the dimes in the apron that he had on. Then he put an "out of order" sign on it.

Well, I cashed in all of the dimes for folding money, which turned out to be twenty-three dollars with a few dimes left over. I thought that railroading wasn't too bad after all.

The next morning, we started for Elko, Nevada on a Macado steam engine. We were hitting about sixty miles per hour when I smelled something burning. Looking out the side, I couldn't see anything. But it kept getting worse and worse till the hog head thought it best that we stop to see what was the matter.

Well, it was a lot worse than we thought. We had four hot boxes on the engine. (That is when the bearings run out of grease and the friction cause heat, which, in turn, causes what grease there is left to catch on fire.) What had happened was that someone in the roundhouse had failed to grease them.

We eased along till we came to a siding where there was a phone and the hog head called the dispatcher to see what he wanted us to do. He told us to wait till another engine could be brought out to us. I never got so tired of waiting in all of my life.

We sat there for ten and a half hours waiting, but that was part of railroading, I guess. They finally got there and fixed our problem so that we could get into Elko.

This was a turn-around point and we rested there. This same crew was to head back. While they were all resting, they started to drink and when it came time for us to go, the train crew was all drunk except for one brakeman and myself. He told me to take the tail end. He would take the head end. If anything happened I was to pull the air, and he showed me what to do.

The conductor and the two other brakemen were in the caboose with me. The hog head was almost out of it, but the fireman hadn't had too much to drink, although he'd had a nip or two. But he was sober enough to run the engine. I am sure if the right people had known about this there would have been some fur a-flyin'.

I was scared to death riding back there with two drunks and I didn't know anything about running a train. The fireman whistled for a high ball from the rear end and I gave him a high ball, that was to say that we were all on and ready to go.

The train started to move and there was a lump in my throat. I felt as if I had a tiger by the tail. There was one thing in my favor, however. Those drunk men were out and a-sleepin' peacefully, and it looked like they would be for quite a while.

I crawled up in the cupola and was a-watchin' so that there were no hot boxes. I didn't understand the train orders too well and didn't know what some of the abbreviations meant, but I had faith in the one brakeman at the head end to do all of the thinking for the two of us.

The train would jerk so much at times that it would nearly knock me for a loop if I wasn't ready for it. Once, when this happened I looked down on the floor and there was the conductor sprawled out on the floor by the barrel of water that was on the caboose for drinking and washing purposes.

Well, he laid there for a few minutes and I was a-hopin' that he would stay there and go back to sleep so that I wouldn't have to bother with him, but he got up and staggered over and picked up some old orders that were a-layin' there and tried to read them.

He was so confused that he was about to pull the air on us. Then he changed his mind and went to the barrel of water to get himself a drink. He got the dipper and bent over the barrel. At that very moment, the train gave a jerk. The conductor lost his balance and he went head first into that barrel of water. He looked like a duck a-divin' for a bug in a pond.

I jumped down from the cupola and I thought that he was going to drown before I could get him out of there. I finally had to tip the barrel over to get him out. He came out of there a-sputterin' and a-coughin' and a-tryin' to get his breath. To say the least, this certainly helped to sober him up a little.

By the time we got back to Stockton, the whole bunch of them were pretty well sobered up and we got the train in without any mishaps. Boy! Home sure did look good to me.

I rested for about ten hours. Then the call boy came and said that I was to go to Oakland next. I was to stay there for a week and learn about the railroad down there.

It was a forty-eight car train and we were to pick up a helper engine at Carbona to push us over the Altamont Pass. Then we were on our own the rest of the way in to Oakland.

On this trip there was a student fireman, myself, two brakemen, a conductor, and the engineer. We called this hog head Casey. That was his nickname because he delighted in scaring all of the students under his direction. As we were going down the west side of the Altamont Pass a-headin' for Oakland, he had her wide open and didn't slow down for any of the curves. The student fireman was a-holdin' on for dear life. I will admit that is was a little rough and I was a little concerned at times, myself.

We didn't have any stops before we got to Oakland and as soon as the train came to a stop I was supposed to go throw the switch to go into the yard. Out came that student fireman and the last I saw of him he was still a-runnin'.

We were making short trips to Hayward and the rock and gravel pit. The conductor was Les Henry, a prince of a man with as much patience as Job. At least, with me. I sure pulled some bad boners.

The morning we were in Hayward, we had set a couple of cars at the poultry spur. There were about ten cars all together. We stopped in front of the depot. Les cut three cars loose from the rest of the train. Then he told me to shove them into the poultry spur, set the brake, and come out with the other two cars.

We had to go up a ways to get on the siding, and while I was a-doin' this, Les went into the depot. We were coming down the siding at a pretty good clip and I gave the hog head a kick signal. I pulled the pin and let them go. As soon as I did this I realized that there was no one on the cars. I was on the engine. I held my breath as I watched them a-goin' down the track. I was afraid that they might hit a car and jump the track. I knew that I could not catch them even if I had tried.

As they passed the depot, Les saw them and he came a-flyin' out and grabbed the rear car. He climbed it like a cat and went to work on the brake as fast as he could, but he was a little too late to stop it before it ran off the end of the spur and across the street. Then it stopped. I felt like doing what that student fireman had done a couple of days earlier, but I knew I would feel better if I took a good chewing out.

When Les got everything in order, he came over to me and said, "Do you know the difference between a shove and a kick?" and he gave me a little demonstration by shoving me a little, then he kicked me in the seat of the pants.

He was just thankful that it was no worse than it was. I was sure nervous and wished he had done more than that.

The next stop was the winery and while we were in getting a car of wine, I threw the switch as we came out. That split the switch and we almost had a wreck right there. We had to call out the section gang to fix the rails and we held up all train traffic for about three hours. You know, he was still not mad at me. I would have run away if there was any place to go. I was sure disgusted with myself and was a-thinkin' that I was not made to be a railroad man.

On the way back to Oakland, Les was real kind to me and he encouraged me to stay with it. He said that I would get better. The next day I split another switch coming into the yard, but this was not so bad as the first one was.

It was some time after that before I made another boo-boo. I was as clumsy as I could be. I was always falling and stumbling. But by now I had caught on to a lot of the sign language they used on the railroad and this was real important. It is a language of its own.

Now I was ready to go back to Stockton. I had finished my training to be a brakeman. It's a wonder that he passed me. I guess with the war a-goin' on, they really didn't have much choice.

Any how, it was good to be back home again with my little wife and boys.

We had just gone to bed. I hadn't gotten to sleep yet, when there came a knock on the door. Yes, that is right. It was the call-boy a-tellin'g me to go to work at midnight and that was only two and a half hours away. I tried to get a little sleep, but didn't do a very good job of it.

We were to go to Oroville on a fast freight with a load of army supplies. We had the right of way over all trains from Stockton to the Oroville yards. I thought that this would be a good run. I was already sleepy as I could be and there would be nothing to do all the way up there and I could rest most of the way.

That is exactly what I did till we got to Craig. There we picked up orders from a train that was in the siding. They read, "Stand by and wait in the siding at Craig till further notice."

The sun had come up good by now and we all decided to take a little nap. We slept till noon and still there were no orders.

We had a lot of fun a-playin' around by throwing rocks at fence posts, watching the pheasants in the farmers field, and most everything we could think of, till one of the brakemen looked at his watch and said, "Do you realize that in ten minutes we will be dead." (That is an expression that we used when we had been on duty for sixteen hours.)

So the fireman put out the fire and we waited till they brought out another crew in a taxi cab to take over. The taxi took us all in to Oroville. It was nine o'clock in the evening.

We were all rested and wanted a little excitement, so one of the guys said, "Let's all go to the Chinaman's and play a little lottery."

I reached in my pocket to see how much money I had and all I could find was a dime. I had forgotten my wallet and had left it at home. As soon as I knew this, I got hungry as a bear. I hadn't thought much about it before.

I said, "That leaves me out. I have only a dime."

Somebody said, "Well, you can mark a ten cent lottery ticket and you might get a buck or two." So I went along for the fun of it. I couldn't eat on ten cents, anyway.

The fellow who was with me said, "I think I'll put a couple of bucks on it." Then he changed his mind and said, "I can mark them spots as good as you can. I'll let 'er ride like this."

They had a drawing every hour on the hour and we didn't have very long to wait.

This is how the game went. There were a hundred numbers on the ticket and you could mark ten of them. If you matched five or more, then you start winning, and, of course, the more you got right the more you would make. I was not very excited about it and was about to leave the place before the drawing. The fellow that was with me said to stay to see if I won something.

"You never know. You might get lucky, " he said.

I said, "If you get lucky and win, can I borrow fifty cents from you to get something to eat?"

"If I get lucky," he said, "I'll buy your supper."

He didn't win anything, but when he looked at my ticket he said, "Look here, Swan! Look at what you have! Go and get your money." So I went over to the window where the Chinaman was a-standin' and I shoved it in to him and he shoved me out $18.75. My eyes were as big as dollars. I thought that he would give me a couple of bucks, if that much.

Then I said to my friend, "Come on. I'll buy you your supper."

He said, "What did you get?"

So I showed it to him and he asked, "Is that all he gave you?"

"Yes," I answered, "Isn't that enough?"

"No, I should say not. You should have gotten $187.50. Why that dirty so-and-so. Cheating you that way." he said, "Let's you and me go back and show him your nine spots and make him give you the rest of your money."

Well, I was tickled with what I had and I was afraid to go in there again. Arguing with the guy might start a fight and I didn't want to wind up all beat up. So I just kept on a-walkin', and we went over to a Chinese restaurant and got ourselves a good Chinese dinner for the two of us.

It was a good thing that I won all of that money for I would not have had any place to sleep that night except in the caboose on the floor. Now I could sleep in a bed and it sure did feel good.

The next morning I went down to the J.C. Penney store and bought a dress for Mama and a play suit for each of the twins. I still had money left over after that.

We left for Stockton about noon. I was riding the head end. We had forty-eight cars and were going along fine. We were to meet a freight, #73, on the siding at Craig, which we did. They were carrying the green. This meant that there was another part to this train a-coming'.

We didn't have orders from it so the hog head said, "Swan, you get off and go call the dispatcher and find out what about this other train that's a-coming' and then pick up the caboose when it comes by."

Well, I tried to get the dispatcher on the phone, but never could. I could hear the train a-pickin' up speed and it was starting to go pretty fast, too fast for me grab hold of it. I couldn't figure out why it was going off and leaving me away out there. I thought I ought to make a try at grabbing it anyway so I got up close to the train and was about to make a grab for one of the box cars as they passed by. But I decided it was going too fast for me.

I thought I'd better wait for the caboose to come by. When the caboose got near the train was a-goin' awful fast, but I didn't want to get left, either, so I made a grab for the front of it. I caught it all right, but my feet slipped on the gravel and there I was a-holdin' on for dear life. My feet were a-bouncin' and a-hittin' the ties and almost going under the caboose. I knew if that was to happen that I was a goner. I had to do something and do it fast.

I decided to let go. I fell away from the train and rolled down the bank as soon as I hit the gravel. The conductor heard me fall and he grabbed the air and this stopped the train.

He ran over to me and said, "**SWAN!** Are you hurt?"

The bill of the cap that I was a-wearin' had slipped over my face and kept me from getting my face all skinned up, but my ankle was a-hurtin' real bad.

I said, "My ankle is hurting pretty bad."

He helped me to the caboose and got a bucket of water and told me to soak my foot in it.

He gave the head end the high ball, but the train didn't move. Then he started for the head end to see what was the matter. About thirty cars from the head end, they found that the draw bar was broken.

Now they had to fix it, and that is a big job. It took about four hours to fix it. And all this time I was a-sittin' there with my foot in a bucket.

When I finally got home, I said to my little wife, "If this keeps up I'm a-goin' to come home with a leg a missin' some of these times."

So I decided to transfer to the switch yard in Stockton. At least I would not have to go out of town and be away from my family so much.

I was a-doin' fine switching in the yard, at least, till one foggy night. It was so foggy that I could barely see the lantern. We were switching in the lower end of the yard. Along in there somewhere there was a low switch. I had stumbled over it before in the daytime and I was a-watchin' for it this night. I was about five cars from the engine and had to cut out five on the end. So I got on where I was to made the cut. The train wasn't moving very fast. At a good walk I could keep up with it. When I got a hold of the hand rails on the box car, my feet were knocked out from under me and my lantern went a-sailin' through the air in a spinning fashion. I managed to get my feet under me and was a-runnin' as fast as I could to keep up with the train for I was between the box cars and if I made a bad move I would go under. There was no way to get out of there. I ran along for the space of three car lengths, I guess, when, all of a sudden the train stopped.

A cold sweat came over me and I was about to pass out with fear of what might have happened to me. As I went over to get my lantern, the engineer came up behind me and threw his arms around me and hugged me.

He cried, "I killed one man that way and if I had killed another, I would die myself. I'm so glad that you are alive and didn't get hurt."

The more I thought about the narrow escape I'd had, the more scared I got. It was so bad that I even dreamed about it.

The next night I was supposed to go on the midnight shift so we went to bed early so I could get some rest before I went to work.

As we talked about the situation, I said to my wife, "Sweetheart, I'm afraid if I go to work tonight, I'll get killed."

She said, "We don't need this kind of a job for you. It's too risky. Go down there right now and quit."

I got out of bed and put my clothes on and went down and quit before I was supposed to go to work. I never went back again, and that was the end of my days working for the railroad. I had worked for them only four or five months. That was enough!

Chapter Eighteen

WORKING IN THE SHIPYARDS

After I quit the railroad job, I soon found another one in the war industry. Pollock's Ship Building Company was brand new, located in Stockton's inland seaport. Most of the people who worked there had just about as much experience as I did, and that was none.

They hired a few men who knew what they were a-doin' and they taught the rest of us. I hired on as a shipwright. That is a different word for carpenter. The only difference that I could see was that we worked on ships instead of houses. We were building wooden mine-sweeps. On our side of the shipyard they were all made out of wood. On the other side of the shipyard they were made out of steel.

I had been working at the Pollock Shipyard for only about a month, I guess. I was helping build the ways for the ships to sit in. On this particular morning, I had just gone to work and went over to the tool room to check out all of the tools that I needed for the day. Among them was an air driven drill that we hooked up to an air hose. A big compressor supplied the air for all of the power tools that the men were a-workin' with.

When I checked this drill out, the man in the tool room said, "Swannie, be careful with it. It's not a-workin' as good as it should, but it's the only one that is left."

At the time, I didn't think anything about it and went on about my business. It had a three quarter inch drill bit that was eighteen inches long. I put it in and was a-drillin' holes in some two by fours that were a-settin' on a couple of saw horses.

The very first hole I drilled, when I was a-pullin' the bit out of the hole I tried to shut the drill off, but all it did was to reverse its direction. As it did, the bit caught the fly of the white carpenter overalls that I had on and the first thing that I knew, it was tearing away at my flesh and it was a real vital spot, to boot.

I didn't have a hankerin' to become a steer, and I got it loose from there in a hurry. But as I did, it took a new hold of me and went into my left leg as high up on my leg as it could get without going into my groin and that thing was eatin' away at me for all it was worth.

I don't know to this day how I stopped that drill, but as soon as I did, I dropped my britches to see what damage was done. As soon as that cool November air hit that wound, I started to really hurt. That is when I started to holler.

One of the workmen who was near by came over to where I was and he looked down at me a-layin' on the cold ground and said, "You poor guy! You poor guy!"

This made me mad and I said, "You fool! Can't you see that I am hurt bad? Go get some help and get me to the first aid station."

It was not too long till there was a crowd of men around there, and all of them were a-wantin' to help me. Well, they very gently put me on a stretcher and took me to the first aid station. They laid me up on a table and started to take off all of my clothes. Blood was running everywhere.

Most of the help they had in the first aid station were young nurses and they seemed to take delight in taking off my clothes. As soon as one of them saw my wound, she went and got some paper towels and started to wipe the sawdust and shavings out the wound. When she did that, I liked to went through the ceiling and I swung at her. If I had made connections she would have been on the floor.

Among all the confusion, I could hear in the distance, a siren, and it was a-gettin' louder all of the time. It wheeled into the gate and I was loaded into an ambulance and I was on my way to the hospital.

Just as we were a-goin' out the gate of the shipyard, I felt like I was leaving this earth. I didn't want to go just yet for I had two little boys that I wanted to raise and a good wife that needed me. I looked over at the man that was a-ridin' in the back with me to steady me when the ambulance went around corners. I asked him if I could hang onto him 'cause if I didn't I thought I'd be a-leavin' this earth. As soon as I got a hold of his hand, I felt like I could stay here, at least for a while. Well, we made a pretty fast trip to the Dameron hospital.

We got there about nine o'clock in the morning. I was taken off that stretcher and put on a table. Some one said for me to start a-countin'. I didn't know what the devil for, but I did as I was told and all the further I got was to eight or nine.

The next thing that I knew, it was late in the afternoon and Mama was by my side. I tried to talk to her, but I couldn't 'cause there was a safety pin stuck through my tongue and fastened to my hospital gown, I guess to keep me from swallowing.

(Daddy only thought he had a pin through his tongue. It was the trachea tube they had left in after his surgery. We didn't have recovery rooms in those days, and they let me be with him right after his surgery.)

Mama pulled it out for me and as soon as she got that out, I told her not to cry, that I was going to be all right.

Then she asked what was the matter with me. The doctor hadn't told her anything except that I had been hurt. I pulled back the sheet and showed her. I was still a bloody mess.

I said, "I sure do hope I didn't lose any of my vital parts," and I made a check the best that I could through all of the bandages. Everything was still there as far as I could tell. The doctor told me later that the only thing that saved my life was the flexibility of the main artery going down my leg.

Well, I stayed in the hospital for several days. While I was there all of the men that I worked with took up a collection for me. I guess there was three or four hundred dollars. They gave it to Mama to hold us over till I got back on my feet. That made me feel real good and I recovered from that pretty fast. I think I only had to stay off work a couple of weeks or so, but when I went back they gave me another job.

The first morning back they took me over and introduced me to a man by the name of Clarence Twining. He was the wood ship caulking boss. The only thing was that he didn't have any men to boss except me. He told me that I was the first one in his new crew and he would be a-gettin' more as time went on. As soon as he got his full crew, he was going to teach everyone how to caulk.

In the meantime I was having a lot of fun going all over the place and looking at all of the things that interested me.

I was glad for this break 'cause I was still pretty ouchy and didn't feel like working real hard. This was fun for about two days, then I wanted to go to work. So I helped him get his school set up and every day or two more men would come till he had his full crew. We spent the next eight weeks learning how to be woodship caulkers. It was a fun kind of a job.

I enjoyed working with this bunch of men. There were a lot of different personalities there. We had butchers, cowboys, farmers, etc. I had been a city bus driver before that.

We were always a-pullin' pranks on each other. It was a cold December morning when we were a-workin' on one of the mine sweeps, a-caulkin' it. There were several crews a-workin' on different levels of scaffold. I was on the bottom level and just above me was another crew a-workin'. In that crew was a man we called "Poddy". That was not his real name, but all of us had a nickname. He was always a-doin' something to me. It seemed that every time I turned around he had tricked me again. I could never catch him in the act.

I had a habit of taking my sweatshirt off when it got too warm to wear it. I would lay it over the guard rail of the scaffold and when I would go back to get it, it would be nailed down with so many nails that it would be all but ruined.

On this particular morning I figured he was going to do it to me again, and I had on a new sweatshirt. I took it off and laid it on the guard rail, just the same way that I had done in the past. I made out like I was a-goin' to the rest room, but instead, I went up on the next level of scaffold and got a five gallon bucket of water that had a skim of ice on it. (There were barrels of water all over the place in case of fire.) I went above where my sweatshirt was a-layin' and waited for Poddy. I didn't have to wait long when here he came with a handful of nails and a hammer. I let him put one nail in the shirt, then I let him have it with this big bucket of ice water right down his neck.

He let out a howl and looked up and saw me. He was real mad and started for me, but I had the jump on him and out run him for a while till he finally caught up with me.

He said, "I'm a-goin' to whip your #^@!".

I said, "Before you do, let me ask you one thing. Would you like it any better whipped than the way it is now?"

He looked at me and there was soon a smile over his face. He stuck out his hand and said, "Let's be friends, Swannie." We shook hands and from then on we were good friends.

I worked there till about the end of 1944. It had begun to look like the war would be over before too long and they were cutting back on the building of ships and I got laid off.

The war had been a-goin' on for four years and I still hadn't been called up for the draft. Maybe now I would be.

Jerry, Jimmy, and Charlotte
"helping" Daddy

Walter is seated in the lower left corner.

Chapter Nineteen

HAM, BACON, AND CHARLOTTE

One evening, a few months after my accident in the shipyard, me 'n Mama were a-talkin over what was the best thing to do with the big sow. It was way past time to take her to the boar and she was so big that we were afraid that even if she did have another litter of little pigs, she might lay on about half of them. Besides, we just had half an acre of land and the neighbors didn't like the smell too well. So we decided the best thing to do was to take her to the slaughter house so we could have some pork to eat.

She was way to big for me to try to butcher by myself with the limited equipment I had. Getting a trailer to haul her in was out of the question, too. We had just enough gas ration stamps for me to get to work, and that was all. So there was nothing else left for me to do but to walk her to the slaughter house.

One morning I decided that this was the morning to do this little job. It was not too far, only about three or four miles. So after breakfast, I went out to the pig pen and fed her. While she was eating I tied a rope around her back leg and waited for her to finish eating.

I tore part of the pen down to let her out. I was not too sure if I could handle her with that rope around her hind leg or not, but she didn't put up any objections to the rope and we were off to the slaughter house a-walkin' along the side of the road.

After a little while she had it figured out what I wanted her to do and it was just a matter of following her all the way there. Everybody that passed us would wave and laugh or honk their horn. It seemed like it took a long time, but we finally got there.

When we got to the slaughter house, all of the men there started to laugh. They had never seen anything like that before. They couldn't believe it.

I felt bad about the whole thing. She was so good to do

everything that I wanted her to do. But we needed the meat. Meat was something that took a lot of ration stamps and it didn't take any if you had your own to butcher. It wouldn't be long till we had pork in the frozen food locker which was right there where they did the slaughtering and butchering. I told them to cure up the hams and bacon and package the rest as pork chops, roasts, and sausage.

I was going to have Mama come and get me, but if she did, I might have to walk to work. The gas was getting low in the car. I had plenty of time, so I started out on foot a-goin' back the same way I had come over, a-carryin' the rope with me. About half way home I got a ride with one of the neighbors.

I soon got over feeling bad about taking that sow to the slaughter house when I started a-thinkin' of all the good ham, bacon, and pork chops. There would be enough pork to last us a long time and that would be GOOD eatin'.

That was the first and last time I ever walked a pig to the slaughter house.

This happened when Jimmy and Jerry were about two years old. After waiting about two or three weeks, Daddy brought home some of the bacon and ham. I think that just one ham must have weighed thirty or forty pounds. That was the biggest ham I ever saw. Daddy put some of the bacon on to cook just as soon as he got it home. That beautiful aroma started to fill the house.

Then, Oh, Oh! I began to get sick to my stomach and I knew for sure that we were expecting another baby. Daddy had to eat every bit of that four hundred pound hog. I couldn't eat a bite of it!

While I was waiting for our baby to arrive I did a lot of resting and reading to the boys. I also knitted each of the boys a bathing suit and some baby "soakers" for the new baby.

Dr. Peterson was away at war and I couldn't go to him so I went to see Dr. Mc Neal. He charged us only fifty dollars for prenatal care and delivery. I was spoiled by Jimmy and Jerry's early delivery, so all of November I kept hoping that the baby would be born.

Finally the time came, but when I got to the hospital the nurses couldn't find my doctor. They kept telling me not to push, but I couldn't help it. Then the doctor arrived just in time to catch the baby. It was a girl! She arrived on November 28, 1943, the day before she was due. Daddy had asked for boys the first time. This time it was my turn for a girl.

Since the two boys had been named after their grandfathers, we decided we'd better name our girl after the two grandmothers, using my mother's first name and Daddy's mother's middle name. So now we had added Charlotte Elizabeth to our family. It sure did seem like a big long name for such a little girl.

Now Jimmy and Jerry had a sister and we were a family of five.

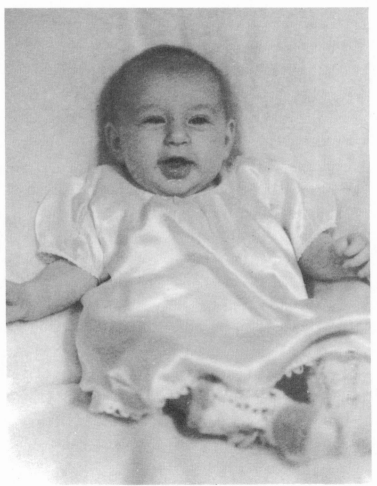

Charlotte Elizabeth at three months

Charlotte at eighteen months

Chapter Twenty

A TRIP TO ARIZONA WITH THE TWINS

It was in late July that my brother, Henry, pulled his 1936 Plymouth to a stop in front of our house on Carroll Avenue. He had an inquiring look on his face as he walked to the house. I was out in the front yard a-mowin' the lawn, but I was anxious to find out what was on his mind. It was not long till my curious mind was satisfied.

"Walter," he said, "Do you want to go to Arizona with me? I am going to see Daddy. You can help me drive and I will pay your fare back on the train."

"Hey! That sounds good to me," I answered, "When do you want to go?"

"Oh, within the next few days, if I can," he said.

While I was talking it over with Mama, the two boys were a-listenin', and as soon as the word was mentioned that I was going some place, they wasted no time in letting their wants known by each of them hugging a leg, looking up at me, and asking to go with me. They always expected to get to go where their Daddy went so they could be with me. It was hard to say no to them. I didn't want to disappoint them.

Mama said, "Why don't you go see your dad and take the two boys with you? I'd like to go too, but I can't with a new baby on the way. I can get some rest while you're gone." And so it was decided that I'd take the boys with me.

Well, we left a couple of days later. It was a little on the warm side, but didn't get too bad till we got a little on the other side of Yuma. Then it got downright hot. Even the car got hot. I had taken all the clothes off of the boys that I could and still have them be a little bit decent.

We pulled over to cool the car off by an irrigation canal so we could get some water for the radiator. While Henry was getting the water, I thought that it would be a good idea to cool off the boys, too.

So we went over by the canal and, one at a time, I held onto them and dipped them into the water while the other one sat on the bank and waited his turn.

When they were thoroughly wet we went back to the car and were on our way to Bisbee, Arizona where my dad lived. We got there the following day about noon.

My dad was so glad to see us all that he even wiped a tear from his cheek after hugging the two boys. We had a very good visit and talked way up into the night, catching up on all that had happened since I had left home some years before.

The next morning came in with a beautiful sunrise, and the smell of dew on the chaparral had a fragrance all of its own. There is no smell in the world that could beat it, unless it was the smell of home cured bacon a-comin' from the kitchen while my dad was getting breakfast for us. I think he must have been saving it for a special occasion and this was it – having his grandsons there with him.

We ate a hearty breakfast and went down to the garden to work a little and to see all of Grandpa's cows and whatever else he had that was of interest to the boys. I got more joy out of watching them with their grandpa than I did visiting with him.

Well, we stayed there for a week, then caught the evening train out of Bisbee Junction, and we were on our way back to Stockton.

The train was not crowded till we got to Phoenix. Then from Phoenix to Los Angeles. It was almost standing room only. We were lucky to have a seat with the war a-goin' on.

I helped the boys get comfortable and they went right off to sleep. I thought I wasn't getting any sleep, but I guess I must have gotten some sleep 'cause I was awakened the next morning by a black soldier asking me if I had lost my wallet. I felt for it and it was gone. Then he held out a wallet in his hand and I saw that it was mine. I offered to give him a reward, but he refused. I was sure happy to get it back.

We had an eight hour wait in Los Angeles. So while we were waiting we went over to the barber shop and got a haircut and shoeshine. That is, I had my shoes shined, then the boys were put out 'cause they didn't get their shoes shined, too.

We went back to the depot to wait some more. We still had a long time to wait, and I was glad when the boys got sleepy and took a nap on the seats beside me, one on each side of me so they could lay their heads on my lap.

They were really a-sawin' them off when here came this same black soldier that had found my wallet. He was so drunk that he could hardly stand up. But he came over to where we were. He was belligerent and said I owed him one. He wanted me to go buy him a bottle of liquor. I knew if I did I could get into trouble. At that time it was unlawful to buy booze for any one in uniform.

After sizing up the situation, I figured that it was best to tell him that I would as soon as the boys woke up, hoping that they would sleep a long time.

Well, it worked! When they did wake up he was gone. I was a very relieved father about that time.

When the train finally came, we got on, but it was so crowded that we had a hard time finding seats together for the three of us. There were three empty seats, all right, but they were all in separate places. It was a worry to me. I had to keep the boys close to me.

As the porter passed by I pulled two dollars out of my pocket and said, "Can you find us three seats together?"

"I sure will try, sir," he said.

It wasn't long till he was back and had it all arranged in the next car. It was well worth it, for we were still a long way from home.

When we got to Fresno, I got off the train and called Mama to come and get us at the Tracy depot. When we got there, she was there and we were sure glad to see her.

That was a hard trip. I hadn't realized what a job it is to take care of a couple of little boys twenty-four hours a day. I never tried to do that again.

Jimmy feeding Jerry watermelon.

Chapter Twenty-one

COUNTRY LIVING

One evening after supper, me 'n Mama were a-talkin' about our family and how we would like to get a little place in the country to raise our kids. She suggested that we look in the newspaper, to see if there was anything in there that we might be able to buy. She soon saw one.

"Look at this, Daddy." she said, "Here is a ten acre place on Alpine Road." We didn't even know where Alpine Road was.

So I called up the realtor who had it listed and we made the arrangements to go to see it the next morning. He said that he'd pick us up and show it to us.

Mama got the boys and the little baby ready and was ready to go when he got there and we all went in his car. It was not too far from our place, about five miles or so, about halfway between Stockton and Linden.

It was a beautiful ten acre place. At that time it was all planted in tomatoes and they were just getting ripe. It was being farmed by an Italian farmer by the name of Victor DeStephani. He lived across the road from this place.

There was not a house on it, but it had some walnut trees. Mama and I fell in love with it and we wanted to buy it. We asked him how much they wanted for it and he told us that they wanted thirty-six hundred dollars for it. They wanted eighteen hundred dollars down and the rest at thirty dollars a month.

I said, "We'll take it!"

I took out my last paycheck from my pocket and endorsed it and gave it to him for a deposit to hold it for us. The check was for seventy-eight dollars and some cents, and he gave me a receipt for it. On the way home, we told him that we that we wanted to sell our place on Carroll Avenue, so he listed it for us.

The next day, the owner of the ten acres wanted to give us our money back 'cause they said that they had listed the ten acres too cheap. But they had already made the deal and it had to stand. We had thirty days to come up with the rest of the money for the down payment.

Well, our place on Carroll Avenue sold right away and we had our down payment money, but we had only thirty days to move out. Now this was scary! Where would we go? We had to find some place to rent, and in a hurry, 'cause there was no house on the ten acres that we were buying.

Mama's folks said that they would fix up an old chicken house on the back of their place that we could move into till we could find a better place to live in.

I don't know how long we stayed in that reformed chicken house but within a month or two we got word of a place to rent out on Alpine Road for fifteen dollars a month from Victor DeStephani, the same farmer that was farming the place that we were a-buyin'.

It was a real old redwood frame house, at least a hundred years old. We all called it "the old fashioned house". It was cold and drafty. It had no bathroom. The worn wooden floors were bare. The only heat was from a wood cookstove in the kitchen, and that was the only room we could heat. The war was still on and we couldn't get propane. The only running water was at the kitchen sink and it was cold – no water heater. But at least it was close to our new Alpine Road place that we were a-buyin'. We could go over there and work on it when I was not working. So we rented the old house for fifteen dollars a month.

The day we chose to move into the old fashioned house was a dark, cold, drizzly, rainy day. It was the middle of November. But we managed to get all packed and moved by the end of the day. We just packed things into boxes and put them into the "new" house then fell exhausted into bed that evening.

The next day Daddy had to go to work early in the morning. The weather was still cold and drizzly. I was left alone with two small boys and an almost one-year-old baby girl in a cold house piled with boxes of things that needed to be put away. The kids were fussy and unhappy in their new and unfamiliar surroundings. And I was pregnant again by about seven months, the baby being due in February.

The floor level between one of the bedrooms was one step down to the living room. I sat down on that step and bawled. It seemed like an insurmountable problem. I don't know how I got through that day, but that evening Daddy decided I needed some help so he called his youngest sister, Rosie.

Rosie's husband was a sailor and was away for the duration of the war. They had a little three-year-old girl, Julie Ann. They were living in Berkeley with Grandy, Daddy's mother.

Daddy asked Rosie if she would come and stay with us until after the baby was born – and she said she would! Grandy brought them over a a week or two later.

We soon settled down to a regular routine. Rosie and I enjoyed each other's company and the kids all got along very well together.

(Rosie told us about an incident when she was baby-sitting for us. She said that she told the boys to do something, but they didn't pay any attention to her. After she repeated it three times, in exasperation she said, "Can't you boys understand English?" They replied, "No. We're Americans.")

We had an unusually wet winter. The house sat back off the paved road quite some distance. Several times we got stuck going out or coming in. There was a much shorter road at right angles from the house which met a road along a railroad right-of-way at the side of the property line.

The only problem was that there was a neighbor who didn't want us to use this road, so he dug a ditch across our road so that we couldn't get to the one along the right-of-way. It was railroad property, but he thought he had exclusive rights to it.

Daddy went over to talk to the man and explain our need to be able to get out quickly in case I needed to get to the hospital, but it didn't make any difference to him. He still didn't want us using "his" road. We never did know why. So Daddy just filled in the ditch so we could use it. The neighbor dug it again! They almost came to blows over it and we didn't want that to happen.

We decided that the best thing for me to do was to go stay in town with my parents until the baby arrived since Rosie was there to take care of the other kids.

I guess it was a good thing we did because the baby put in her appearance just a day or two later. Our fourth child, another girl, was born on February 8th 1945.

Dr. McNeal was my doctor again this time, and almost the same scene took place as it had with Charlotte's birth. He charged us his usual fee of fifty dollars.

We named the baby after a beautiful girl I knew when I was going to school. I thought she had a beautiful name. It was Carol Jean Swan. (We later got reacquainted when she heard about our book, "me 'n Henry".) By this time we realized that we were giving our kids names with double consonants. Jean didn't have them. (We didn't think of spelling it Jeanne.) So we named her Ann instead. We have always called her Carol Ann. Never just Carol.

When she was about a month old, Rosie and Julie Ann went back to Berkeley. She had helped us much more than she will never know and we are thankful for her.

Carol Ann at six months, Aug. 1945

Ten months

First Birthday

With Mama at 13 months

About two years.

Carol Ann's Page

We were still living in the old fashioned house when the war was finally over. Daddy had to work nights. That wasn't very satisfactory because with four kids in the house it's impossible to sleep during the days. He quit that job after a short time and began to see if he could find any work plastering.

It seemed that it took all that I could make to just feed the family and there was little left over for anything else. So getting a house built and a well drilled was a major undertaking. But we did get started on in and we did what we could.

Mama drew some simple house plans and I bought a load of hollow-tile 12"x12"x4" blocks for the walls of our new house. Many was the time that Mama would put the new baby in the buggy and wheel her over to the house I was a-buildin'. She would put the baby on the side of the house where there was not so much wind and help me with the work. The boys even helped as much as they could as little as they were. Sometimes, it looked impossible to ever get it built. But, like a lot of other things, it did get built.

During the building of our house on Alpine Road, Daddy met an elderly gentleman, a Mr. Jones (not his real name) who needed someone to stay on his ten acres while he was going to be away for about six months. He offered us his place, rent-free, if we would live there and tend the sheep he had there and fix up his house a little. He even gave us the money to fix up the house and to pay Daddy for his work. He said that he was going to Chicago and wouldn't be back for six months. This looked like a good deal to us, so we moved from the old fashioned house over to his house about two or three miles away towards Linden. This was almost a year after we had moved out to the country.

This house was small, but it did have a bathroom and hot and cold running water. We had to put our bed in the living room and Carol Ann's crib there, too. Charlotte had a cot in the hallway and Jimmy and Jerry slept on a mattress in a room up over the back porch. They had to climb up there on a ladder. We had our dining table in the kitchen.

Daddy was very busy at his work. We wanted to get our own house ready to live in just as quickly as possible, so he spent as much time as he could working on our own house so that it would be ready when Mr. Jones returned. He didn't get any of the improvements to Mr. Jones' house done.

About three months sooner than we expected to see him, Mr. Jones came back. When he saw that we hadn't done anything with his house he got mad as a wet hen. We weren't home (at his house). We were at our house working on it. Mr. Jones got into his car and drove over to our place on Alpine Road.

He came storming up to where we were working and started to shout at us about our not fixing up his house first. He got so mad that he took a swing at Daddy, but he was a very short little man and missed. Daddy just took him by the back of his coat collar and the seat of his pants and carried him out to his car and told him to leave. Daddy didn't want that kind of language used around his family. Before Mr. Jones left, he said that he was going to get a gun and shoot all of us. Needless to say, we didn't want to take any chances.

I went to the corner store and called Mom and asked her to come out as quickly as she could and get the kids. She and Dad got there in minutes. Daddy and I, and my father went to Mr. Jones' place and got everything we owned out of his place within two or three hours. Mom kept the kids overnight and Daddy and I slept in our new unfinished house for the first time.

We never saw Mr. Jones again.

We had been working on the house for more than a year. The doors weren't hung, neither the outside nor the inside was plastered, and the bathroom was only a small room with no shower or toilet. But it was ours and we did have a roof over our heads even if we had to use an outhouse again. It wasn't too long until we were pretty well settled down again. The best thing was that we were once again living on our own property. We didn't have to worry about pleasing someone else. And our lives moved on.

Charlotte and Carol Ann helping Dad Robinson

Dad and the kids working on our house

Chapter Twenty-two

THE DRAFT CAUGHT UP WITH ME

It was while we were still a-livin' in the "old fashioned" house on Alpine Road, and shortly after Carol Ann was born. It must have been about the middle of March of 1945.

I had just gotten home from a-workin' at the Clover Leaf Milk Bottling plant when Mama greeted me at the door.

She said, "Honey, you have a greeting from the President of the United States."

"What does that mean?" I asked.

"Well," she answered, "It means you are being called up for a physical examination to be drafted into the army."

I was to be at the Greyhound bus station early the following Monday morning to go to Sacramento for this physical examination. I sure did a lot of thinking and worrying about it.

Well, Mama took me to the bus station, and there were a whole lot of other guys there besides me. They looked kinda worried, too. After a while we were loaded into six Greyhound buses and headed for Sacramento.

When we got there we all gathered in a big room. We were put into groups of twenty. Then each group took its turn a-goin' from one room to another. In the first room we took off all of our clothes except our shorts. Then we lined up to get inoculated. Then we went, one by one, to the next room and sat down where there was a funny looking doctor a-sittin' behind a desk. All he did was to ask a lot of dumb questions. At least, they sure sounded dumb to me.

Then we were ready for the next room. In here we all lined up in single file, side by side, facing in the same direction. The doctor went down the line giving each of us a once over.

When he got to the end of the line he said, "That's all. You can get dressed now. Go get in that other line."

97

This time another doctor walked down the line and asked each one of us some more questions. One of them was, "Do you know of any physical problems that you have?"

When he came to me and asked me this question, I told him about my back injuries a few years back.

He said, "Yeah, that is what they all say. What proof do you have of all of this happening to you?"

I reached in my pocket and pulled out the doctors report that stated that I had a twenty-seven percent disability and handed it to him. I was sure happy 'cause Mama had saved it for me, and she made sure I didn't forget to take it along with me.

Now this put a different expression on his face, and he said, "You go stand over there in that other line."

There were three of us in our group of twenty that were told to stand in that "other line", and we were sent to another room where there was about thirty or so men. We were asked some more questions, and I was told to get into another line. We waited there for so long I began to wonder what was a-goin' on.

Finally, a soldier came in and said, "That is all. You can go. Get on the bus and go home. You will get your notice in a few days."

It was real quiet on the bus all the way back to Stockton, nothing like the noise that was a-goin' on when we were headed for Sacramento.

Mama was at the bus station to pick me up when we got back to Stockton. She wanted to know all about it, but I couldn't tell her much because they hadn't told me anything about what was going to happen.

About a week later I got a card in the mail with a new classification on it. It was "4-F"! That meant that I was not physically fit for the army and I would not be drafted. What a big relief this was!

It relieved my conscience. I was not a draft dodger. I just did not qualify for the armed services.

Besides, it was a lot more fun being a husband and a daddy.

World War II was over six months later!

Chapter Twenty-three

THE BIG WHITE HORSE

While we were still a-livin' on Mr. Jones' ten acres, Jimmy and
Jerry and I went to French Camp one day to a livestock auction.
We went there most of the time just for the fun of it. I always liked
to listen to the auctioneers chant and to see what the market was
on livestock.

The first thing that ran through was the horses. I had it in the
back of my mind that it would be helpful if I could pick up a good
horse to cultivate with, even though I didn't know very much about
them.

The last horse that went through the ring was a dapple gray
mare, as pretty as a picture, fat and shiny. There was nobody a-
biddin' on her at all, so I bid eighty-five dollars and as soon as I did
the auctioneer said, "SOLD!" I was pretty happy. Now I had me a
horse!

As I went to pay for her, there was a man came up to me and
asked,"Do you have any way to haul her?"

I said, "No."

"Well, I'll haul her for you for five dollars." And I took him
up on it.

When we took her out of the trailer when we got home, she
was as gentle as a kitten. I had me a good horse!

Well, I had to go to work that week and it was not till the next
week that I had a chance to try her out to see what she could do.

In the meantime I had borrowed a set of harnesses from a
neighbor. I harnessed her up and hitched her up to an old sled that
I had there.

I said,"Git up!"

She did not hear me, I guess. I said it again and still nothing
happened. Then I swatted her across the back side. She jumped a
little. Then I did it again.

All this did was make her mad and she swung around and headed at me. She reared up on her hind feet and came at me a-pawin' her front feet in the air.

By now I had no control over her at all and I was a-lookin' for a place to get away from her. I started a-runnin' and saw a dead old oak tree a-layin' there on the ground. Somehow I got on the other side of it, but the horse tried to go through it. She got the traces tangled up in those old tree limbs, and that slowed her down enough for me to get away.

Mama heard the confusion and came out into the backyard with Charlotte a-followin' her. They could see what was a-goin' on, the two of them were as scared as I was.

I was about THAT close to going into the house and getting the deer rifle and shooting her and calling the tallow works to come and get her, but instead, I waited till she cooled off a little, and I put a leather halter on her.

Mama asked, "What are you going to do? Stay away from her. She'll hurt you." But I was careful.

I took all of the broken harnesses off of her and said, "I'm going to take her back to the auction sale and see if I can get my money back for her."

"How are you going to do that?" Mama asked.

"I'll lead her behind the car. If you'll drive it, I can hold on to her halter from the back seat."

I got out a one-inch rope and tied it around her neck just in case she threw another fit.

It was still early and we had plenty of time to get to the auction sale.

Mama put all of the kids in the car and we started out. I had a hold of the lead rope that I fastened to the halter. The other rope, I tied to the car with some slack in it, just in case. I told Mama to drive very slow and she never took it out of low gear.

Well, everything went along just fine till we got about halfway there. Then that big white horse decided that she was not going to go any further. She planted all four feet firmly and started to skid. The halter broke. Then the rope came around her neck with a jerk so hard that it stopped the car.

Mama started it up again and put it in first gear and started to move. That horse skidded along for a little bit. Then she started a-walkin'. I told Mama to go a little faster so that she had to trot a pretty good clip. This worked and we never stopped again till we got to the sale barn. By that time the horse was pretty well lathered up with sweat.

The sale had just started and by the time that I got all of the paper work done and they ran her into the ring right away. I told them to sell that big white horse as is.

I said, "What you see is what you get."

There were a couple of truck farmers who saw her and they started a-biddin' on her. They both wanted her and when they were through, they had bid her up to twice what I had paid for her in the first place. I was in luck this time.

I went and picked up my check and we all went home a-feelin' pretty good about the whole thing. From then on I stuck with tractors to do my cultivating. It would be a lot safer for me that way.

This is a good place to tell you a couple of stories about Charlotte. She witnessed the incident with Daddy and the big white horse. We didn't realize what a trauma it was for her until a little later.

Her bed was just a small cot in the hall near the bathroom. One night she began to scream in the middle of the night.

We jumped up and ran to her. We were really worried. The boys had never done that and we couldn't imagine what could be the matter. We tried to comfort her, but she wouldn't settle down. I don't know how many minutes this went on, but finally she stopped crying enough so we could understand what she was trying to tell us.

She thought there was a horse in her bed and it had frightened her. We pulled back the covers and showed her there was no horse, but she wouldn't get back into her bed.

We tried bribing her, but that didn't work. It seemed that nothing we could do would get her back into that bed. So we finally gave up and said that she could come and get in bed with us. She even refused to do that until we pulled back the covers to show her there wasn't a horse there. Even then, I had to hold her close and love her until she went to sleep.

We, as adults, don't realize the terrible trauma children may go through, triggered by an event that we probably wouldn't think about much. We are able to forget it in a little while, but their young minds don't know how to handle it very well. It was a long time before she would go to bed without checking for that horse under her covers.

Charlotte was a thumb-sucker. Not only was she a thumb-sucker, but she was also a hair twister. She would suck her right thumb and twist her hair with her left hand. She did this so much that she began to get bald spots on the top and back of her head. It also make her hair thin and straight and straggly. She was two years old.

Daddy and I were discussing what we could do about it. I sure didn't know. But he came up with a solution. He thought that if we cut all of her hair off, at least, she couldn't twist it. By the time it could grow back in maybe she would have broken the habit and wouldn't do it again.

So with reluctance, I consented to such drastic measures. And Daddy cut it! <u>ALL</u> OFF!!

I refused to take her anywhere until it had grown enough so that you could tell she <u>did</u> have hair on her head.

We found out that that was a pretty good solution to the problem. Her hair came back thick and beautiful. But she still sucked her thumb for another year or two. She never really broke the habit of twisting her hair, but at least she never got bald spots again.

Charlotte's Haircut

Chapter Twenty-four

JERRY BROKE HIS HEAD
AND OTHER TALES

I started to do down to Orvis and Clingers frozen food lockers for some frozen meat. As soon as all of the kids heard where I was a-goin' they wanted to go, too. So the whole family wound up a-goin', even Mama.

All the transportation that we had then was a small flat bed Model A Ford truck and whenever we went any where, the two older boys had to sit on the back on some boxes that we put up against the cab. They were given strict instructions to sit down all of the time, and most of the time they did pretty well.

Well, I got the meat out of the locker and we headed for home. There was a short steep grade up to the paved road, and I stopped to check for cars a-comin'. I looked back and saw that Jerry was standing instead of sitting. I turned my head to tell him to sit down, my foot slipped off the clutch, the truck jerked, the motor died, and Jerry was pitched off!

I jumped out to see if he was hurt. He seemed a little dazed, but he didn't look like anything serious was wrong with him, so I put him back on the truck.

We stopped at the corner grocery store to get some bread, I looked at him and he still looked dazed and pale, but I thought he was all right.

That night he threw up several times. By morning we knew we'd better call the doctor. He said to bring him in immediately.

Well, they took an x-rays of his head and found that he had a hairline crack in his skull and he had a concussion. The doctor wanted to put him in the hospital. He said that he needed to be kept in bed for a month.

The sounds of this scared me. I said, "Can't we just keep him in bed at home?"

The doctor said, "It's pretty hard to keep a young active boy in bed."

But I assured him that we could manage just fine. So the doctor let us take him home. When we got there the rest of the little kids ran out to the car to greet us and to see how Jerry was and learn what the doctor said.

Well, we all went into the house and I told them that Jerry had a concussion and had to stay in bed for a whole month. The only time that he could get up was to go to the bathroom.

I looked over at Jimmy and said, "Since Jerry is your twin brother, it is your job to take care of him and keep him company and make sure that he stays in bed."

Then I said to Jerry, "If you stay in bed all of the time and do exactly as you are supposed to do, as soon as you are well, I will go down town and buy you a brand new bicycle for Christmas."

And I spoke to Jim, "And if you see that he does not do anything that he is not supposed to, I will buy you a bicycle, too."

After I had told them I would get them both a new bicycle, I started a-worrin' about how in the world I was a-goin' to get enough money to buy two new bicycles.

We didn't have a television in those days to entertain them, so Mama got them some coloring books and small toys to keep them busy, but quiet. She also read to them.

Well, Jimmy did his part and Jerry did his part to keep the bargain, even if the time did seem to go by real slow for them. But for me, the time went fast and it was upon me all of a sudden. It took all that I had a-comin' from a plaster job to buy those two bicycles.

We decided to buy full sized bikes because the boys were growing so fast we knew that they would soon be big enough to ride them, but it did make it a little hard for them to learn to ride.

As soon as we got home from the bicycle shop Jimmy helped Jerry to learn to ride his bike and Jerry helped Jimmy. They had a lot of fun times a-ridin' together. I can't count how many times they rode to the corner grocery store to get some little thing for their mother.

Jerry never had any bad effects from that fall on his head. They kept those bikes till they wore them out.

One day Daddy and I started to go down to the corner grocery store about a half mile away. We were going to take the kids with us, but Jimmy and Jerry wanted to stay home. They were getting big enough to be responsible if they were left alone for a half hour or so. So we loaded up the little truck with the smaller ones.

Just as we had backed onto the road, here came Jimmy running as fast as he could and hollering as loud as he could. Daddy quickly pulled back into the yard to find out what was the matter, and here came Jerry holding his hand out in front of him. It was bleeding!

There was no trip to the store then. We had to take Jerry to the emergency hospital in town.

Jimmy and Jerry had decided that they were going to cut down the big sunflower in the garden, and that required a sharp knife. Jimmy had the knife and Jerry thought he wasn't doing it right and tried to take the knife away. He ended up having to have seven or eight stitches in his left fore-finger. He's carried the scar ever since.

One day one of them complained about his foot hurting. When I examined it, I could see that it was very swollen and red with infection.

I took him to see Dr. Mc Neal. The nurse and I helped give him ether so the doctor could lance it. (Now-a-days the doctor would use a shot of novocain.) Then I had to carry him going down the elevator and to the car. By that time he was a pretty big kid and it wasn't very easy for me to carry him.

A week or two later the same thing happened to the other one. A week or two after that, same thing happened to the first one again, except this time it was in his hand. And that wasn't all! A week or two later, the second one had another foot infection. With each of these events we had to use the ether and I had to carry those big kids back to the car. Talk about fun!

Because Jimmy and Jerry's birthday was in April and the Glenwood School didn't have a kindergarten at the time, they had to wait until they were nearly six and a half years old to start school.

They were so big that I had to buy size twelve blue jeans for them and cut about six inches off the legs. That was before they made slim, regular, and husky jeans. They wore the horizontal striped tee shirts –size twelve.

By this time they had learned to ride their bicycles, and they rode them to school.

They entered the first grade the third day of September 1947. We didn't know that day that we would have children in elementary and/or high school for the next twenty-four years.

The New Bicycles

Jimmy and Jerry's First Day of School
with teacher, Miss Roush

Chapter Twenty-five

ME 'N THE BOYS WENT FISHING

It was the time of the year that the stripped bass were a-runnin', meaning that they were a-comin' up from the ocean. It was a time that everybody went out to try their luck. That was all that I heard where I was a-workin'. Some of the men that I worked with wanted me to go with them, but I thought that it would be a lot more fun if I took my two boys with me.

I had taken Jimmy and Jerry bank fishing with me from the time that they were real little, but both of them wanted to go out boat fishing and I figured that they were big enough. So Mama fixed us up a big lunch and we got up real early one Saturday morning and headed for the river.

There are a lot of rivers in that part of the country where we lived. Some of them ran together and that was where the best fishing was. There were a lot of boat docks where you could rent a boat.

When we got to where we wanted to go it was just about daylight. We figured that if we were early we could get a good boat. But we were out of luck. They were all gone except for a little one. It was not very good and it didn't have any life jackets in it.

I was just about to go find a good place on the bank to fish, but the boys looked so disappointed that I lost my better judgement.

Well, the tide was just a-comin' in and it was quite a chore to row that boat against the tide to get out a little ways where we wanted to do our fishing. I decided to anchor the boat where there were some tullies. I figured that there was a lot of good fish there. So we fished there for a little while, but didn't catch anything.

By now the tide had slowed down so that I could go 'most any where we wanted to, so I rowed to another place and anchored there. We were a-catchin' a lot of fish here. Some were big ones, too. Then, all of a sudden, the wind came up. The tide had changed and was a-goin' out. The waves were getting real big, and every time that a speedboat would go by we had a hard time a-stayin' in that boat.

I started rowing back for the boat dock, but the tide was so swift that I couldn't make any headway at all. I was getting scared, so I threw all of the fish overboard and everything else that I could to make the boat as light possible.

Then the thought went through my mind, what if we were to tip this boat over? What would I do? I could not hold on to both of the boys and swim, too. I was getting panicky. We were a-driftin' away from the boat dock all of the time.

Finally, I maneuvered the boat over where there was some tullies and we tied on to them. I figured that we could stay there and wait till the tides changed.

Now this fishing trip was not fun any more. I thought, if I ever get back to the dock, I'll never go fishing in a boat again.

Every once in a while there would be a speed boat come by and I would hold on to those tullies for dear life.

After a while another boat came by, but this time the man saw us and slowed down a little. I thought, now this is a lot better.

Then he stopped and drifted over to us and asked, "Are you in trouble?"

I said, "I sure am!"

He said, "Would you like for us to tow you to the boat landing?"

"That would be wonderful!" was my answer.

It was not long till we were on the boat landing. I felt like kissing the ground when we were walking to the car.

When we got home, the first thing Mama said was, "Did you catch any fish?"

One of the boys said, "We caught a lot of big ones, but Daddy threw them all back in the river."

Then I had to explain what had happened to Mama. She was as scared as I was.

Now, after all of these years have passed and I think about it, I can't believe that I used such poor judgement and yet nothing bad had happened.

Chapter Twenty-six

BROWNIE COW

By now we were all settled in our own little house on Alpine Road. The family was getting a little bigger and it was past time to get a milk cow. I had heard about a dairy that was going out of business over on Fairchild Lane, so me 'n Mama and the family went over to have a look at what there was for sale.

We got there at milking time. I guess there were at least ten cows to choose from. The man who owned them was very nice to us. He went along the row of cows a-tellin' us about each one of them.

Then he came to this particular one. She was a Jersey and gave good rich milk, though not a lot. She was a first-calf-heifer and would probably give a lot more milk the next time she had a calf.

We asked the man what he wanted for her and he told us he'd take one hundred and twenty-five dollars. That was about what they were going for, so we bought her. The next day he delivered her to our house.

We didn't have any place for her, so we kept her tied up with a rope and moved her from time to time, as soon as she would eat up all the grass around her.

She didn't have any horns except for a couple of crumpled nubbins where they had tried to dehorn her when she was little. The kids named her Brownie because she was brown.

The two boys would come out with me when I went to milk and would sit there on a box and talk with me all of the time that I was a-milkin'.

One day Jerry said, "Daddy, how big do I have to be before I can milk?"

I said, "Well, I guess you 'n Jimmy are big enough right now."

So I got up and got another box and put it on the other side of the cow. I showed them how to milk and stayed there to give them a helping hand if they needed it. I was a-standin' there ready to give instructions.

They said, "Daddy, We can do it. You go to the house. We can do it ourselves."

"If this is what you want, I guess that's the thing for me to do." I said. And I went into the house.

It was not too long till here they came in with about two inches of milk in the bottom of the milk bucket and said, "We're all finished!"

Well, Mama took the milk and strained it and bragged on them for being able to milk the cow. But before she washed out the milk bucket, I handed it back to the boys and said, "That's fine, what you have done. Now take the bucket out and get the rest of it."

Both of them went out again mumbling something I couldn't understand.

As soon as they were out of hearing Mama said to me, "Don't you think that was being a little hard on them, Daddy?"

I will have to admit that I did feel a little bad, but I knew that they could do better and I said, "No, if you don't expect more out of them, every time that they go out to milk, they will not get all of the milk. Wait a little while and see what they do. If they can't do it, I will go help them."

It wasn't long till they came in with the rest of the milk. Of course, we bragged on them and said that we were real proud of them.

I think that Brownie Cow liked those boys 'cause she would just stand there and chew her cud and wait for those boys to get through milking.

I strained the milk into a big two-gallon pan and put it in the refrigerator. There was hardly a meal that went by without a big pan of milk sitting on the table, and most of it would be gone by the end of the meal. I even fed the babies with Brownie Cow's milk.

I seldom skimmed off the cream. I just stirred it up and we all drank as much as we wanted of that good rich milk. We didn't know about cholesterol in animal fats not being good for your health then. Now we are paying for our ignorance.

110

We never ate cereal with milk or skimmed milk. We used CREAM! In the summertime we always had lots of ice cream made with plenty of cream in it.

Whenever Brownie Cow was "dry" (not giving any milk), which was usually about six weeks to two months before she was to have a calf, we all missed her good rich milk, and we were always anxious for her to be giving milk again.

Well, we kept her for all eight of the kids. They drank her milk every day until she got pretty old and feeble. When she got to old to milk any more, I found a place where I could turn her out on pasture and she could go and come as she wanted and live out the rest of her life. I would take her a little grain every day.

One day, when I went to feed her, she did not come up for her grain. I went a-lookin' for her. I found her in a ditch. She had fallen and had broken her leg. When I walked up to her, she mooed. To me it sounded like she was a-sayin', "Please help me. I am hurt."

I went to get someone to help me, but when we had gotten back she was dead.

We had a lot of cows after that, but there never was another one that gave as good milk as she did. We missed her when she was gone.

Jimmy and Jerry

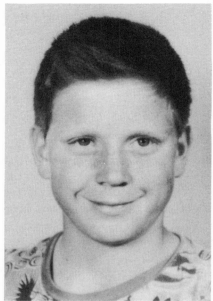

Jimmy, seven years old.

Jerry, seven years old.

Chapter Twenty-seven

MY PLASTERING CAREER

This was the day that I decided that I'd have to make a little more money than I had up to this point. So I started out to look for a job as a plasterer. I threw my tools of the trade in the back of the car and started out looking for a building that was being plastered. I looked for a long time and was about to give up and go home to try it another day, but on my way home I saw a store under construction. There was a plaster mixer standing there with a pile of sand beside it. So I pulled over and went in to see the man who was in charge.

When I asked him for a job as a plasterer, he said, "Are you a plasterer?" I said that I had done a little of it, but I was a fast learner.

Then he said, "Get your tools and get up here on the scaffold and start spreading. The boss told me to hire anybody that came along because we are short-handed and you look like anybody."

As soon as I started to plaster I could see that I was not a plasterer because he was plastering twice as fast as I was.

Soon he looked over at me and said, "I thought that you said that you were a plasterer."

I said, "No, but I wanted a job as a plasterer."

He said, "Well, you can stay on the job till the boss comes back in a day or two and let him decide whether you stay or not."

I tried my best to keep up, but I was always behind and he had to come and help me. This went on for three days till the boss showed up on the job.

As soon as he saw me working he went over to me and said, "You're not a plasterer, but I will give you half of journeyman's wages."

I could not feed my family on this amount of money so I told him that I was a lot better now than I was the first day and I could not work for that amount. I picked up my tools, got my check, and started for home.

The first traffic signal that I came to, a car pulled up beside me waiting for the signal to turn green. The driver looked over at me and motioned for me to pull over. He said that he wanted to talk to me. So I pulled up into a vacant lot where we wouldn't be in the way of the traffic. He got out of his car and introduced himself as Louie. He was a builder and he had ten houses that were all ready for plaster. He said he would give me double the plasterer's scale if I would do them for him and I would be paid at the end of every week. I told him that it would take me about a week before I could get started on them. And we struck a bargain.

After he left, I sat there in the car for a long time trying to figure out what I should do. I knew that it was too big for me to tackle all alone. So I turned around and went back to job I had just left. I was going to talk to the boss to see if I gave him this job, he would hire me. But when I got there he was gone, and it looked like the job would be finished in a day or two so.

I talked to Hershel, the fellow that I had already worked with. I told him that I would hire him for double the plasterer's scale as soon as he was through with that job if he wanted to work for me.

He said, "For that kind of wages, I'll work for you."

As it happened, he had a plaster mixer and some scaffold, just enough to get by with.

About this time, in came the hod carrier and I said, "Henry, do you want to go to work for me? I will give you double what you are a-makin' here." He was excited and was ready to go right then.

We started a week later on this project. As slow as I was, we were falling behind, so I hired two more plasterers to help us. They were real good plasterers. All three of them had a lot of compassion for me and they showed me a lot about plastering. I was a learning fast.

I thought this was a good business to be in. I decided to go and get my contractor's license. There was a whole lot about the plastering trade that I did not know. I found that the hardest thing that I had to do was to meet the payroll at every end of the week. But I managed to keep going, learning as I went.

When our two older boys got up old enough that they could help, they were anxious to work with me. So I let them work on

114

every job that I could. That is, until the union business agent came on the job one day and said that I was violating union rules, that I could not hire my two boys to help me, and that if I did not hire a union plasterer, they would put a picket line on my job.

Now this angered me a lot and I said, "That is fine. When is this to take place?"

He said, "In the morning."

"Well, if this does take place in the morning, I will picket the union hall with my wife and all of my little kids. I will make them all a sign and I'll call the local newspaper to tell them that the union is unfair to a man that has eight kids to feed. I'm teaching them a trade."

I was interrupted at this point and he said, "Well let's talk about this a little."

I said, "There is no talk necessary. Either you let me teach my boys or the whole country will know about it." At that point he got into his car and drove off and that was the last I heard of him.

When I got home that evening, there was a phone message for me from a contractor who wanted to see me about a job. I was to meet him in his office at eight the next morning. I had never done any work for him. As soon I saw what the job was I was scared because it was so big. It was the Masonic Temple building. It had had a fire and there was a lot of water damage.

I told the man that it was a lot bigger job than I could handle, but I would give him a bid for insurance purposes.

He said that would be fine, so I spent several hours looking and measuring and I didn't know any more when I was finished then I did when I had started.

So I just picked a figure out of the air and said, "It will cost you one hundred thousand dollars."

He thanked me and I left his office figuring that was the last of it. I went on a-doin' a few patches and other work.

One morning he called about ten and said that I had the job and asked when I wanted to start. I was surprised and scared at the same time.

I said, "I still can't do this job for you. I have a whole house full of kids and have no money to run a job as big as that."

Then he said, "Come on down to the office. I want to talk to you." I said I would, but that wouldn't change anything.

Well, the next morning I went down to his office and we talked for a while. He asked me if I knew how to do this job and I said that part did not bother me in the least. It was the money part that was the trouble.

Then he said, "If the money problem was solved would you do it?"

I said, "Yes, what did you have in mind? You know that there are a lot of contractors in this town that have the money to do this job for you." And I named a few.

Then he said, "Well, this is true and how did they get their money? We know how they got it. We have spent a lot of money investigating all of the plastering contractors in this town and we know who they owe and how much. We are looking for a man with integrity. You are the one we want to do our work. We will work with you any way that we can so that you can do the job.

"Now this is what we propose. We will give you this job on this basis; time and material, plus twenty-five percent above all costs and you will get a check every week."

I had never heard of this before and it sounded to good to be true, but it was.

Well, I called up the plasterers union hall and ordered out six plasterers and four hod carriers and told them to be on the job ready to go to work at eight on Monday morning. That morning I got them all together and told them that I was going to pick a foreman for the job. This would be done the next Friday as soon as I could see how they worked and what their qualifications were to do a job like this. I never told them that this was a time and material job. The production was unbelievable that I got out of those men.

The man that was in charge of the job for the Masonic Lodge was so surprised that he made this comment, "How in the world do you get that much work out of those men?"

I said, "If you get good men and leave them alone they can sometimes do a better job than if you are riding them all of the time."

Well this job went real smooth. I appointed one of them foreman and gave him more money – enough to make it worth while. As long as he got the work out he kept his foreman job.

It was not long till I learned a lot of tricks from the men and

116

became a better plasterer myself. By then the word had gotten around and we did another job for a funeral home on the same basis. All of this taught me a lesson. No matter what career you are in, you soon come to know exactly what you are. For most of my life since then, that was how I made a living for my family.

My advertising sign on a plastering job. Our motto was "From the smallest patch to the finest home."

117

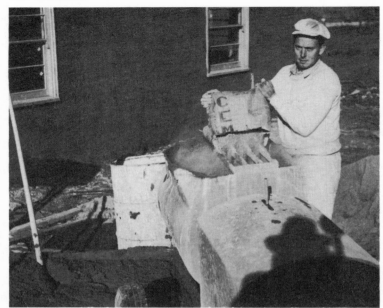

Walter

The Plastering Crew

Chapter Twenty-eight

ALLEN

We had been a-livin 'on our own ten acres on Alpine Road for about two years. I didn't have much time to do any farming 'cause I had to work in town just to put groceries on the table. Mama was pretty busy with the little ones, and to top it off, Allen, our fifth child, wanted to come and join our little Swan family. But we weren't just too sure if he would make it 'cause Mama had a lot of trouble. She had to spend some time in the hospital and take it real easy till he arrived.

I hired a black woman by the name of Mrs. Fraizer to look after the little ones while Mama was in the hospital. She was really good with them and the little kids loved her. She always had supper on the table when I got home from work. She was a good cook, along with being a down right good person.

It seemed that I could barely just make enough money to get by on – almost. I don't think that we would have made it if it was not for the fact that Mama felt the way she did. The little baby's came first. If they needed something, they got it before she thought about a new dress or something for herself.

I remember the day Allen was born real well. We were a-workin' on a house close to Oak Park. Claude DeMasters was my hod carrier and I had sent him out to the house for some more material. He came back without it and said that my wife needed me. So we all took the day off and I took Mama to the hospital for Allen's arrival.

Allen weighed over eight pounds when he was born, but he soon became kind of puny. He didn't eat real good like the rest of the kids did, but with a lot of loving care from Mama he came out of it.

The winter of 1946-47 was a difficult one. We had a lot of rain and fog. This little house we had built of hollow tile blocks (and still hadn't finished – no bathroom) held the dampness and the walls in the kids room were getting mildewed. All four of them slept in the same little room in bunkbeds with the boys on the top bunks and the girls on the bottom bunks. If one of them got a cold, they all got a cold. One of them came down with the measles, then all the rest of them did, too.

Then, to top it all off, by springtime I was going to have another baby, but this time all didn't go so well. I was sick the whole time I carried Allen. It was a difficult time for all of us. Daddy was beginning to feel the pressure of owning his own business and the need for going out to find work to keep his men and himself busy.

We had planned to name the baby Robert Allen if it was a boy. Then shortly before Allen's birth we took our little family to see Lucille and Del, who were back in our area. Their youngest son's name was Robert. They called him Bobby. He was full of life and vim and vigor and mischievous as all get out.

When we got home I said, "I'm not naming any of my babies Robert if all Bobby's are that ornery." So we changed the name to Walter (after Daddy) Allen. Then we had to decide just what we would call him because we didn't want to call two people in the same family by the same name. So it had to be Allen.

(We didn't know it then, but this caused us some problems later. Henry and Ruby had named their son, born nine months earlier, Alan. We never dreamed that one day Henry's Alan Swan and our Allen Swan would both be in the same school room for a year or two. It was a little confusing for their teacher.)

When the time came for Allen's birth, his delivery went well and he seemed to be a big (eight pounds fourteen ounces) healthy baby and we were happy to have him with us.

We didn't know it then, and even for years later, that he had trouble digesting milk, which caused him to be a "puny" kid for years and years. He just wouldn't eat right.

One day when Allen was six months old, Daddy and I had an evening appointment. Mom usually took care of the kids for us when we needed someone. The older kids liked this because they really loved their grandma, but Allen hadn't had much of a chance to get acquainted with her very well.

We were running a little late, so when we got to Mom's house all of the other kids piled out of the car and ran to the house. I ran *carrying Allen to the front door. I literally tossed him to Mom and we left immediately.*

When Allen saw me running away from him, he started to cry. He cried all evening, until Mom took him home and put him in his own bed. Even then, he cried himself to sleep. It was a very traumatic experience for him. We couldn't leave him with Mom for almost a year. He was afraid even when we took him over to her house. Sometimes we parents make some terribly stupid mistakes, and this was one of them.

When Allen was two years old he would be sick a day or two, then seem to feel all right for a day or two. Then he would be sick again. This went of for nearly two weeks. When I finally took him to the doctor, I received a thorough reprimand. Allen had pneumonia!

When he was four years old he looked sick all the time. His eyes looked dark and hollow. Again I took him to the doctor. He said to give him lots of milk and protein. He never examined the possibility that Allen couldn't handle milk and probably couldn't handle meat, either. I didn't know then that there are many people who can't. All he would eat was peanut butter and honey sandwiches. I guess that was the best thing for him under those circumstances.

We didn't learn just what his problem was until he became an adult and had a family of his own.

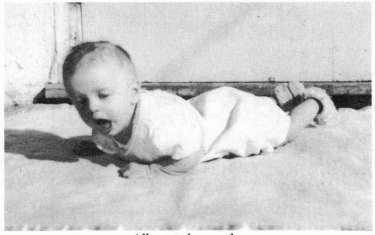

Allen at six months

Allen after his haircut
on the same day.

Allen before his first haircut
on his first birthday.

Chapter Twenty-nine

OUR "VACATION"

It was about the end of June or the first of July in 1948. At the supper table one evening, one of the boys asked me, "Daddy, what is a vacation? The neighbor boys say that you going to have one of them," and that started the wheels a-rollin' after I explained what it was.

We talked about it and decided to take a little vacation ourselves to out to Bisbee, Arizona to see my father. It had been a long time since we had been together. I tried to get him to come out to Stockton to see us, but he never would.

So we loaded up the only vehicle that we had. It was a big dump truck that I used with my plastering business. I made some ribs and put a canvas cover over the back. It kind-a looked like a covered wagon. But it was nice and we had a lot of room for all of the kids. We didn't have so many then. All we had was Jimmy, Jerry, Charlotte, and Carol Ann, and Allen, who was just eight months old.

We started out early in the morning before it got too hot. Sometimes it can get pretty hot in July, so I bought a water cooler that we could hang on the door window. It was like an evaporator cooler that you would have in your house. It was pretty nice if you kept plenty of water in it. Usually one of us stayed in the back with the kids while the other one drove.

Things were going along fine until Allen got real sick about the time we got to Gila Bend in Arizona. We stopped and took him to see a doctor to see what was the matter with him.

The doctor said that he had gotten too hot and he would be all right if we made sure that he was kept cool. He advised us to stay in a motel the rest of the day and travel at night when it was cooler.

But we didn't have enough money for a motel, so we kept on

a-travelin'. I drove and Mama held Allen on her lap and she kept sponging him off with a damp cloth and by the time we got to Bisbee, Allen was feeling a lot better.

We visited with my father and he was very happy to see our little family. Then we down to Palominas to visit with my sister, Hazel and her family. She had a passel of little kids. Her husband worked in the mines in Bisbee while she took care of the ranch. They had 160 acres, a few cows and chickens and a garden. The older kids did the chores such as milking the cows, and whatever.

I thought it would be a fun thing to do if I hid some small change under the milking stool and other places where they could find it. I emptied out my pockets of all the change that I had so that all of the kids that did chores would find some of it.

Forty years went by before I ever heard the outcome of this. The kids found the money, all right and they all thought that they had a real rich uncle. I was glad that it made them feel good.

When we got ready to head for home, Natalie, who was Oliver's wife, wanted to go with us. We knew she could be a big help to us with the kids, so we took her along, too.

We tried to do a lot of night time and early morning driving on account of the heat. We bedded all of the kids down in the back except for Allen. Mama was a-holdin' him and was a-sittin' up in front with me to keep me awake so I could drive.

It was early in the morning and we had been a-travelin' for some time since we had checked on the kids in the back. All of a sudden I saw a good place where I could pull over and I slammed on the brakes and pulled off the road. As I pulled over, there was a big truck a-comin' around the curve from the other direction.

I said, "Mama! Did you see how close that truck came to us? He almost hit us and we were almost all the way off the road!"

I got out and went around to the back of the truck and I saw a big cloud of dust down the hill on our side of the highway. I went down to talk to him.

Almost crying, he said, "Thank God you had pulled off the highway. My left front tire blew out and I didn't have control. Is everyone all right?" He had come around that curve on my side of the road. If I hadn't pulled over exactly when I did, there would have been a head on collision.

The more me and Mama looked at the situation, the more scared we got. Boy! That was too close!

There was not a whole lot that I could do for the truck driver. He had managed to keep the truck upright and all he had to do was change the tire and he could be on his way.

Well, we finally got home okay and it sure felt good to be home again and to take a good bath and rest up from our "vacation".

Later, we were very glad that we had taken the time and money to go 'cause that was the last time I ever saw my father alive. He died the following October.

Here we are as we traveled in the big dump truck that we used for Daddy's plastering business. It was in July of 1948.

Jerry, Jimmy
Charlotte, Carol Ann
Spring of 1947

Chapter Thirty

AN UNEXPECTED TRAGEDY

It was October 25, 1948 and I was a-gettin' ready to go to work. I had just finished eating breakfast when the phone rang. It was my younger brother, Oliver calling from Bisbee. He told me that our father had died that night.

This was quite a shock to me and it took me a little while to get my thoughts together so I could figure out what I was a-goin' to do.

First off the bat, I had to tell the men that were a-workin' for me what had happened, and the best way to do that was to go out on the job. That way I could catch them all.

We were a-workin' on the east side of Stockton on Sinclair Street for a fellow by the name of Meath. As soon as I told him what had happened, he said that he would fly me over to Bisbee if I wanted to rent a plane.

Now this was before there were any regular commercial planes a-comin' in to Stockton and so this sounded like a good plan. I told him I'd make all of the arrangements and that I would meet him at the airport in the morning.

I went home and called my younger sister, Rosie, who lived in Berkeley, and asked her if she wanted to go with me to the funeral. She said that would be fine, so I told her to meet us at the airport in Oakland and we would swing by and pick her up.

Now this was a little Piper Cub, a three seater job. I would have called it a puddle jumper, but it was a lot faster than riding the bus to Bisbee.

In those days the only way you could tell where you were was by radio beams and beacon lights at night. I had never flown with Meath before and knew nothing about whether he could fly or not. But, nevertheless, we were on our way.

We had to stop at a little airport in the southern part of

California for gas and rest a little and get a bite to eat. By then it was a-gettin' along towards evening. I had never been up in the air after it got dark and I was afraid of running into someone out there.

It seemed like we had traveled a long time. I sure didn't know where we were and I sure hoped that he did. All that we could see was some lights down below of some cities.

I kind of figured that by now we should be over Arizona somewhere. I could see that he was a-talkin' over the short wave radio to some one down there on the ground. There was a pair of head phones a-layin' beside me, so I picked them up and put them on my head. I could hear them both a-talkin' some kind of numbers and a lot of letters that I was having a hard time of making any sense out of.

I could tell by the way they were a-talkin' that there was something wrong. It was pitch black under us. Then, all of a sudden, they started talking something that I could understand. We were lost and were about to run out of gas. The pilot was trying to find out how far it was to Gila Bend.

As soon as he found out he said, "That is too far. I don't have enough gas to go that far. Is there any place that I can land any closer?"

The man on the ground said, "There is a landing strip not too far from here, but there are no lights there. All it is a strip that I had a grader cut for me and it is pretty rough. It has a lot of gullies in it and it's not very wide either. If you come in from the north, I will have my pickup head lights on. Land real quick and you'll be okay.

Now, Meath didn't know that I was a-listening to all that was a-goin' on. You can imagine what was a-goin' through my mind. Rosie was asleep and I was glad for that. There was no use for me to wake her and scare her to death, too.

Soon I saw the headlights of the pickup and we were a-comin' down. And not a minute too soon 'cause that airplane was a-startin' to sputter and tell us that was all she wrote. There was no more gas left.

Well, the pilot got it all the way down and brought it to a stop and here came the pickup with a barrel of gas in the back and they filled up the plane.

I was just not too sure that I wanted to continue on to Bisbee, but I finally talked myself into it and we were airborne again. Rosie was still asleep. In fact, she did not wake up till we landed at the Douglas airport sometime after two o'clock in the morning.

There was a fancy looking car a-waitin' for us. It was much to my surprise when the driver said, "I am at your service. Where do you want to go?"

I said, "I want to go to Bisbee, about twenty miles from here. Is that too far for me to ask you to go?"

He said, "No, that's okay. Get in and I'll take you."

I gave the pilot a twenty dollar bill and said, "Go to Douglas and get yourself a room and some sleep. I will meet you at the Bisbee Airport in a couple of days. The old homestead is just east of the airport and you can buzz the house to let us know that you're there."

It was still dark when we pulled into the old homestead and everybody was asleep, but they knew that we were a-comin' and had beds ready for us.

I didn't sleep much the rest of that night for thinking about what had happened at Gila Bend and about my father.

It was sad the way that my father had left this world. He was not feeling too good and figured what was the use of going on any longer. He had had seventy-one years of life and he thought that was enough in this troubled world.

Henry found him the next morning. He called the coroner and they took him up to the Hubbard Mortuary. The cause of death was a self-inflicted gunshot wound.

This grieved me for many years for he was truly a great man. He taught me a lot of good principles of life even though he never went to church a day in his life that I knew of. We got a preacher to be there when he was buried in the Evergreen Cemetery. All five of his kids were there, but my mother didn't come.

As soon as the funeral was over, we met Meath at the Bisbee Airport and headed back for Stockton.

Yes, we got lost going home, too. Somewhere around Daggett the pilot lost the radio beam, but this time I was not so scared. It was still day light and this made me feel a lot better, and we had plenty of fuel left.

Well, Meath criss-crossed till he got on the radio beam and we made it on to Oakland to let my sister off. Then we flew over to Stockton. He went out and buzzed our house and Mama came down to the airport and got me. I was never so glad to see home as I was that day. That was a real ordeal for me and it took me some time to really get over it.

It was some forty-four years later that me 'n Henry got around to putting a head stone on his grave. In fact, we did it today – Sept. 29, 1992.

Chapter Thirty-one

COUNTING NOSES

Shortly after Grandpa Swan died, Henry and his wife, Ruby, and their kids moved to Stockton. (You've read about Henry, Daddy's brother, in our book "me 'n Henry".) Since the little house that we had built for Daddy's plastering buddy was empty, we let them move into it. They had five kids and it was a little crowded, but it was a roof over their heads until Henry could find work and it sure was better than nothing for them.

Although the kids had plenty of room to play on our ten acres, Ruby and I decided to take the kids to the city park in Stockton to play for a treat. It was probably one of the kid's birthday, although I don't remember right now. We had five kids at the time ourselves. We piled all of the kids into our car and headed for the park.

We bought some special treats for them to eat and had a nice picnic. The kids had a lot of fun playing on the swings and other playground equipment, and we all enjoyed our outing very much.

When the kids began to get tired, we gathered them all up and piled them back into the car. Then Ruby and I got in.

Before I started up the motor, just jesting, I said, "Maybe we ought to count noses to make sure we got all of them. Let's see, there's one, two, three, four, five, six, seven, eight, nine. Wait a minute! I'd better do that over again I must have made a mistake. One, two, three, four, five, six, seven, eight, nine. Oh, oh! Someone's missing! Who is it?"

So we named them, "There's Rosa May, Beverly, Sandy, Alan, and Russell. Well, Ruby, all of your kids are here. There's Jim, Jerry, Charlotte and our Allen. Carol Ann's not here! Where is she?"

I jumped out of the car and ran to the playground. There was Carol Ann in one of the small children's swings that had two wide straps crossed to make a seat for the little ones. She couldn't get out by herself. She was having so much fun that she didn't even know we were leaving her stranded there all by herself.

The moral of the story here is; when you've got a bunch of kids you'd better count noses. And it became a habit with us.

Several years later, after we have eight kids ourselves, the kids and I went Christmas shopping with another of my sisters-in-law, Valida. We had all gone into one of Stockton's "fancy" department stores where I usually didn't shop. We looked around for a while and decided we couldn't afford their prices, so all took off to look for another store we could afford. We crossed the street at the traffic signal and I looked around for Linda, who was four or five years old at the time.

There was no Linda with us! We had forgotten to count noses!

I told Valida to hang on to the rest of the kids and I hurried back into the store. I went to the section of the store where we had been just before we left. There was Linda, sitting on a small bench by the fitting rooms. She was crying. One of the saleswomen had rescued her and told her to wait for a little while. She knew that Linda's mother would soon be back.

One of my greatest fears as a young mother was that of losing one of my children. It was not a good feeling for a little while there. You can be sure that for the rest of our shopping expedition Linda and I didn't get very far from each other.

After that experience, I always remembered to count noses. It may have sounded a little silly, but I figure that it's better to be safe than sorry.

Chapter Thirty-two

HOGS AND POTATOES

From the time that I was a little boy I liked hogs. I was plastering a house over on Waterloo Road for some people. They had some hogs there and we got to talking about them. They were wanting to sell them all. They said if I would take them all I could get them real cheap. The hogs were Durock Jersey Reds, a good blood line and to me they looked real good.

Well, we talked for a while after I had finished the plaster job and I wound up with all of those hogs and I marked the plaster bill "paid in full". On Saturday we hauled them all home.

I figured with that kind of pigs I could start me a hog farm, so I turned them all loose in the alfalfa pasture. In a few days all of them were a-holdin' their heads sideways and a-shakin' their heads.

That was the first time that I had ever seen hogs do that, so I called the vet. He came out and looked at them and he said all of them had grass stickers in their ears. We called them foxtails. It is a kind of grass that grows in that area naturally. It heads up like wheat or barley. When the hogs were eating the grass, the foxtails would work their way into their ears.

The vet said that we would have to catch all of the hogs and take the foxtails out. So me 'n the two boys caught them one by one and got the job done. I had to buy a pair of surgical clamps to do the job with. Now we had to pen them up and feed them, and that got real expensive.

I heard that some of the farmers were getting potatoes for ten cents a hundred pounds. So I went out to the potato fields where they were harvesting them. But they wouldn't sell us any. We had to have some kind of a permit from the government agriculture department and pay for them there. So that's what I did.

The way I understood it, it was some kind of a subsidy to help the potato farmers. I never could figure it all out, but it didn't matter a whole lot. We got the potatoes for five dollars for a whole truck load of them.

We started to feed them to the hogs raw, but they weren't doing too well on them. Then our neighbor came over one day and said that he had a BIG cast iron pot over at his house. He said to come over and get it so I could cook the potatoes for those hogs. They would do a lot better with cooked potatoes.

Well, this was a big pot. It would hold two hundred pounds of potatoes at a time. Now this became a daily chore for Jimmy and Jerry – cooking potatoes.

There was nothing wrong with the potatoes. They looked the same as the ones that we could buy in the grocery store except that they had some purple ink squirted on them so that they couldn't be sold in the store. But that came right off as soon as they were peeled.

We sure had a lot of potatoes to eat! Most of the time we fried them, but we also boiled them, mashed them, and baked them. Sometimes I even saw the boys eating them when they were out a-feedin' the hogs.

I had one of the hogs butchered and then we had pork to go along with the potatoes.

Well, the sows started to have little ones. I was a-workin' all of the time, plastering. I didn't have time to take care of the hogs the way that they needed. You can imagine what it looked like there with all those little pigs a-runnin' all over the place. It was a mess!

One day, when I got home from work, there was a fellow with a big truck a-sittin' in the driveway a-waitin' for me.

As soon as I got out of the car, he walked over to me and said, "Do you want to sell those little pigs?"

I said, "Yes, if you want to take the whole kit 'n caboodle of them."

We agreed on a price and he loaded them all up except for one sow that was about to have little pigs. I kept that one so I would have a pig around to eat up the table scraps.

We took the money and paid some bills and bought the kids some clothes for school. And I consoled myself by saying, "As soon as I can get set up right I will try it again," But that day never came while we still had the kids at home with us.

Chapter Thirty-three

THE "BIG" HOUSE

I was a-plasterin' for one of the local construction companies. Frank was the owner and manager of it. One day he called me in to his office and talked to me. He said that I needed a bigger house. Well, he was right. Our little house had only two bedrooms and we already had five kids in the little one. He made it look so easy to get this bigger house that I couldn't resist. All we had to do was sign the papers and he would do all of the rest. He estimated the cost would be ten thousand dollars and it would take him only two or thee months to build it. Then we could move into a brand new house. We didn't see anything wrong with it, so that is just what we did.

He sent his whole carpenter crew out and started building on the house in December of 1948. Whenever he got so much done on it, he would make a draw on our loan. But soon we could see that it was going to take a lot longer than two or three months. I guess he saved our house to work on when he didn't have any other place to send his men. The work and time seemed to drag on and on. Then, one day, he told me that all of our money was gone.

Our new "big" house had the roof on, and the doors and windows were in and the outside of the house was plastered. But, there was no flooring down, (just the sub-floor of two by sixes). There were no bathroom fixtures in, the interior walls weren't plastered, and there were no doors on the kitchen cupboards. None of the rooms were plastered, and there were no French doors to the outside from the dining room. In fact, there were no doors at all there, just a hole. And here it was November 1949, almost a year after it was started.

We getting mighty cramped in our little house, so we decided to move into the big house just the way it was and finish it as we could scrape up the money.

We had two bathrooms, but there were no wash basins in either one and only one of them had a toilet and it didn't work. We had to fill a bucket with water from the bathtub to flush it with. It was quite a while before we got the shower working in the little bathroom.

I put in a make-shift door to take the place of the French doors that we didn't have in the dining room.

We'd had electric heaters installed to heat up the house so that we could live in it, but if we turned them on the electric bill was so high we couldn't pay it. We had a fireplace in the living room and that warmed up the living room, dining room, and kitchen pretty good, but it was a hungry fireplace and it ate up a lot of wood.

Now we had three houses on our Alpine Road ten acre property, which had had no houses when we bought it. We called the first house which we built and lived in the "middle" house. The small one-bed-room house we had built for a plastering buddy, which he never moved into, we called the "little" house. And the third was the "big" house which we moved into before it was finished. It was also the house we were living in when our last three kids were born.

I guess you might say we were "coming up" in the world.

The twins were big enough to cut wood and bring it in for the fireplace. They often complained, "If we bring in more wood, you'll only burn it up and we'll have to go and get more."

One cold, wet, and windy day, with the wind coming from the southeast, we found out that the chimney to the fireplace wasn't high enough. The wind came over the top of the roof of the upstairs room we had over the garage and blew the smoke right back down the chimney. We had to add about four feet more to it to correct the problem before we could use the fireplace.

The front porch wasn't finished. There was no cement floor on it and there were no steps. But there was a good roof over our heads. That part was good!

Before we moved into our "big" house, on February 22nd of 1949, the kids needed some entertainment, so we decided to have a birthday party for George Washington. I made a cake and some hot cocoa, the kids planned some games, and Daddy was going to tell some stories. We were going to have a grand party.

By this time the new "big" house had the room over the garage so we decided that this would be a good place to have our party because it was big enough for them to play in, even though the house was a long ways from being finished enough so we could move into it. We called this room the "rumpus" room. It was a place where they could run and jump if they wanted to. (Later that spring, Daddy put one hundred baby chicks in it to raise them until they were old enough to put outside.)

After having a fun evening, someone suggested that we measure each of the kids on the closet door for a permanent record. We found a pencil, measured each of the kids, and put the date by the measuring mark.

That started a tradition in our family. Every year after that, as long as we lived in that house, we had a birthday party for George Washington and marked the closet door with the kids heights.

One year it was a sad occasion for us. Thirteen days after our youngest child was born she became sick with tracheal bronchitis. We had to take her to the hospital and leave her there, not knowing what was going to happen. We debated about whether to put her height (length when born) on the door.

I said, "Yes, we will! No matter what happens!"

Forty years later, we still have that door. We've carried it with us with each move we've made, and even installed it as a bathroom door in two or three of the other houses we've lived in. Later we measured the grandkids on the other side of it. It was a big occasion for all of us when we didn't see them very often.

Just recently one of our grandsons came visiting, bringing his new bride to meet us. He asked if we still had the door. He wanted to show it to her. They found it out in the shed, but this time we had to put the mark in the middle of his forehead. He was about four inches taller than it was.

Now each of the kids is wanting to inherit that door. It was an important part of our lives. I guess they will have to draw straws for it, along with some other items of sentimental value.

The "Big" House ready for plaster.

Walter plastering the "Big" House

Chapter Thirty-four

MORE STRUGGLES AND GROWTH

We had been a-livin' in our new unfinished big house about six months. Things had been kind of tough for us and we hadn't been able to do much more to the house. We needed the money, so on Memorial Day, May the 30th, 1950, a holiday, all of the men that I had a-workin' for me wanted a day off, but I needed to work.

I had a house out on Milton Road that I just about had finished for Andy S. and he was a-wantin' to move in. So I figured that I could do it myself. It needed the final color coat on the outside. We called it "washing" them. It was more like painting than plastering.

I left home without any lunch and beings as it was away out in the country, I stopped by the little corner grocery store and picked me up a can of sardines and some crackers for my lunch.

When I got on the job, Andy saw that I was a-workin' alone so he helped me. It was the first hot day of the year and it was a scorcher for that time of the year. I had forgotten my hat and my dark glasses. Most of the time when I had a wash job to do I wore dark glasses to keep the wash out of my eyes and to cut down the glare of the sun on that white wash.

I was a-workin' real hard to get finished that day and took just enough time to swallow those crackers and that can of sardines. I just kept on a-goin' the rest of the day. I was about ready to go home when Andy saw that his bull was out in the road and he asked me if I would help him get him back in so that he would not get hit by a car. I was glad to help him. After all, he had helped me all day.

We had a devil of a time with that bull. He wanted to visit some of the neighbors cows across the road and we about ran our legs off trying to get him in.

When we finally got him in the corral, my mouth was so dry that my tongue was a-hurtin' and I had a real bad pain in my belly. I figured that those crackers and sardines had given me indigestion. I felt real faint and so I sat in the shade for a little while. I started to feel like I was going to pass out. Finally I got a little bit better and went home.

I went to right to bed 'cause I was dizzy and my belly was really a-hurtin'. Mama got me a glass of water with a little baking soda in it, but that didn't do any good. I finally dozed off to sleep. But around ten o'clock I woke up with real severe pains in my belly that doubled me over. I was really a-hurtin', and I began to throw up.

Mama called Dr. Peterson and told him how I was acting. He told her to take me to his house, he wanted to take a look at me. Well, he sent us over to the Dameron Hospital and they put me to bed.

The doctor was puzzled as to what was the matter with me. All that I knew was that whatever it was, I wished he would find out what it was and fix it so I would not have so much pain.

They put an IV in my arm and put me in an oxygen tent. In a little while I started to feel a little better. The doctor didn't leave me all the rest of the night.

Mama had to go home to see that the kids were all right, but she came right back after checking on them.

She asked the doctor what was the matter with me and he said that he thought that I had had heat exhaustion and was very sick.

Well, I felt very sick. I don't remember how long that I stayed in the hospital, but when I got out, it left me so that I could not sweat and would get over heated real easy.

It was impossible for me to work for a long time and things started a-fallin' apart at the seams. There was no money a-comin' in and we owed a lot of bills. The collection agencies started in on us. We were swamped with them. Every time the mail would come all of the envelopes had windows in them.

Mama sat down and wrote them all letters saying that we would pay every one of them as soon as I could get back on my feet. Sometimes we had to give them all one dollar a month, and even this was hard to do.

This was the lowest time of my whole life, I guess. It was hard for me to see my family suffer so and I couldn't do anything.

After a while, there was a little plaster job came in and I told

Mama I was going to see if I could go and do it 'cause we needed the money real bad. It was out in the country and I went alone to do it. Mama didn't want me to do it, but I did it anyway.

I would work a little while and as soon as I started to hurting, I would stop and rest until I felt better. Then, all of a sudden, I started a-sweatin'. It was the first time that I had done that since I had gotten too hot. From that day on I started a-feelin' better every day and I could work a little more each day.

Well, we finally got all of our debts paid off, but it wasn't too long till we were back in debt again. Mama was pregnant again, so soon there would be another mouth to feed. It is awful hard to stay out of debt when you spend more than you make. All of those little youngun's sure took a lot of groceries, but some how or another you can pull through if you never give up and you come out a better person after it is all said and done.

Somewhere along about this time childhood diseases caught up with us. It seemed that no matter where they slept, they still managed to get what everybody else had.

Chicken pox was a fun time for them. None of them were sick enough to be totally miserable. They had energy to play and enjoy getting to stay home from school and under my feet.

Allen was still young enough that he had only a very light case of them, but some of the older ones were covered from the tops of their heads, to the bottoms of their feet, especially Charlotte, who was the worst.

We weathered that storm. Every year we'd get several colds and usually the flu appeared sometime or other.

Then, one of them came down with the mumps. Three weeks later to the day, all of the other four came down with them. Jimmy and Jerry were ten years old that year. That was a hard time for me, but before too long they were all well and back to school.

This was the year that Daddy was sick a lot, too. He really suffered from stress trying to keep up with all that was demanded of him. He was still trying to plaster, but during the cold rainy and foggy winter months work was always slow. You just can't plaster when it's raining.

This always made our Christmases less than we had hoped for. It seemed that was to be our lot from our very first Christmas.

Now it was my turn to get sick. I was pregnant again. I didn't have morning sickness. I had ALL DAY sickness. I was hardly able to do anything. I spent a lot of time resting on the couch.

I was just barely able to get the washing done, even with the help of an automatic washer and dryer. But doing the dishes and cooking the meals was another thing. When Daddy got home from work, he would cook the evening meal. They would have had to do without if it hadn't been for him. The big boys learned early to help with the cooking, too.

Charlotte and Carol Ann were seven and six years old at the time. Those poor little girls had to start doing almost all of the dishes for me. It wasn't easy for them. Both of them were too short for the height of the sink, so they stood on a box to make it more comfortable for them. (It seemed that we kicked that stool out of our way for years.) One of the girls washed the dishes on the odd days, while the other one dried them. The other one had the even days. When there were two odd days together, I "caught up" the dishes for them. Those two girls were our main dish washers until they grew up and got married.

I felt really sorry for Carol Ann. She was so slow that it took her hours to do the dishes. If they weren't clean, Daddy would make them do them all over again. We had a electric dish washer, but it didn't get the dishes clean, either, and it was more trouble than it was worth.

After about two months of being VERY sick, the doctor finally gave me a shot that stopped the awful nausea.

Towards then end of my pregnancy, I was so large that we knew I was going to have another set of twins. We had proof when the doctor sent me to have x-rays six weeks before they were born. (We still have that x-ray.) I was happy that we were having twins again, but also apprehensive. That would make seven children for us!

The doctor said they would probably be early. Twins usually are. For the next six weeks, almost every day in the late afternoon, I would feel like this would surely be the day. Then finally, they were born on December 12th, three days before the due date and thirteen days before Christmas. It was an early Christmas present for all of us.

This time we had a boy and a girl. We named them John David and Merri Lou. Both of them were beautiful, normal sized, healthy babies. Johnny weighed seven pounds and ten ounces, and Merri

Lou weighed six pounds and ten ounces. That was over fourteen pounds of babies!

The local newspaper, the <u>Stockton Record</u>, thought this was such an unusual event that they sent a reporter out to do a story about it. Both sets of twins got their picture in the paper with the big boys each holding one of the babies.

We didn't have a way to heat the bedrooms, so we put a crib in the living room for them for the first two months, putting them both in the same crib.

We didn't have ANY money to spend for Christmas and we told the kids that the new babies would have to be their Christmas presents. I don't know if they minded about that or not, but they didn't have any choice, and they accepted it with grace.

Daddy and the bigger boys went up to the foothills and got a Mansanita bush to use for a Christmas tree. We decorated it with what we had on hand.

Then, on Christmas Eve, we saw several cars drive up to the house. We weren't expecting any company and couldn't imagine who it could be. We turned on the porch light and there stood Mom and Dad and my two brothers with their families. They had brought Christmas to us. We were very grateful to them for the kids sakes. We had a grand time with all of us together.

From the time that Jimmy and Jerry were small babies, I took my babies to the San Joaquin County Well Baby Clinic. It didn't cost anything and the babies were checked over very well each time I took them. It was at this clinic that they each received all of the immunization shots and had their weight checked. I felt good about the service I received there.

Then when Johnny and Merri Lou were six months old, they each got a shot which was given to them in the upper arm. Usually the skin would be a little red around the site for a few days, and sometimes they would be a little fussy for a day or two. Shots are never fun.

But Johnny's shoulder began to swell. He looked like a football player with his shoulder pads on. He was fussy and it hurt him for me to pick him up. This looked like it needed a private doctor's attention, so I took him to the doctor who had taken Daddy's appendix out.

The doctor took one look at him and knew immediately what was wrong. *He had a sterile abscess as a result of the shot. Without any pain medication, he used his scalpel and lanced his arm almost at the point of his shoulder. Johnny cried only a little. By the time the doctor had his arm and shoulder bandaged up, he was feeling fine.*

There were times when it seemed like we lived from crisis to crisis. If it wasn't one thing, it was another. But you can't give up. You just keep on doing what needs to be done, almost from moment to moment. Then the rewards come a little later when you are least expecting them.

Jim holding Johnny, Jerry holding Merri Lou

Merri Lou and Johnny at two and a half months
March 1, 1952

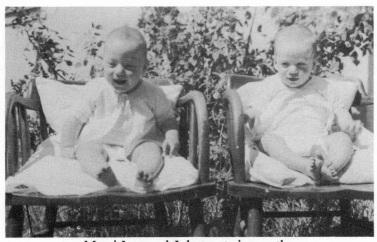

Merri Lou and Johnny at six months
June 12, 1952

Johnny and Merri Lou at twenty months

Merri Lou and Johnny at two years

Chapter Thirty-five

MY K G O T V APPEARANCE

In the early 1950s Henry and his family lived next door to us, and on different occasions, he and his family would come over to listen to me tell stories. One time he said that he had been a-watchin' the TV and he saw a show that would be just the place that I could tell some of my stories on. It was the Bell Brook Milk Show with Armand Girard as host. They were inviting anybody that had any kind of a talent to come and be on their show. It was a fun thing with no money involved. It was in the early days of TV. It was all live. What you did was what was put out on the air right then.

Well, Henry was a-tellin' me that I should try out for one of the shows. I was reluctant 'cause I didn't think I was good enough to go on TV. He kept insisting that I go and try out for one of them.

One day he said, "If I get an appointment for you, will you go?"

I said, "If you get the appointment, yes, I will go."

About a week later, here came in the mail, a card asking me if I could go to Oakland for an audition. Now this was exciting. So I went!

It was a real scary thing for me to do. There were a lot of other people there a-waitin' to try out for the show. Among them was Captain Kangaroo.

After the audition they thanked us for coming and we went home. I figured that would be all of it and I would never hear from them again, but I had a lot of fun doing it anyway.

It was about a week later when here came a card a-tellin' me that I had made the audition and that I should be in Oakland at a certain time to be on the air.

I wanted this to be a real good story, so I wrote one just for

147

the show. It was about a parrot. I went over that story till I had it down pat. I had it timed till it lasted exactly three minutes – just like they wanted it.

The day to perform came and I went over to Oakland. But my confidence flew out the window and I was scared to death when I got there. I was a-wonderin' what I was a-doin' there in the first place.

This was a long time before there was anything like color TV and before they taped what you did before it went on the air. It was exciting and scary, too. I was to be the first one on the program.

There were a lot of bright lights a-shinin' from every direction and there were microphones a-hangin' from the ceiling just out of sight of the cameras.

They had a spot marked on the floor where I was supposed to stand. I was told not to move from that spot. There was a group of Cub Scouts a-sittin' on the floor in front of me and I was to tell them a story. They gave me the que to start a-talkin'.

I was doing fine till I came to the last line of my story. Then my mind went blank. My head was a-spinnin' and I thought for sure that I was going to pass out.

Then, all of a sudden, I thought of what I was to say and it turned out without any one knowing the difference.

I won a little trophy for giving the best performance that time. I still have it.

Another time I went to Oakland again to tell another story. This time I took a friend of mine who was a cartoon artist. He drew the story on white paper with black charcoal as I told the story.

I told my *Teeny Weeny* story that time. We were a big hit and my story became a big hit, too.

Teeny Weeny was a little boy who wouldn't drink his milk and the wind blew him away.

Some years later I was a'tellin' this story to a young family. The next day the wind was blowing very hard. The smallest boy in that family, who wouldn't drink his milk, either, said to his mother, "I think you'd better give me a glass of milk this morning. I don't want to get blown away." His mother had to tell me thanks for telling her child that story.

Chapter Thirty-six

BEANS, BEES, AND STATE HOSPITAL

It was early spring of 1952. I had been a-goin' to the early morning farmer's market to pick up whatever I could to feed our growing family. I heard that Kentucky Wonder Pole Beans were a good crop to raise and was told that they sold well at the farmer's market.

Plaster jobs hadn't been coming in as good as we needed to feed our family. This seemed to be as good a solution as any for making a little more money. So I rented five acres south of Linden near an irrigation canal so we could raise a crop of beans where the soil was good and sandy.

I borrowed some equipment so I could get the soil ready to plant and we all went over to plant the beans. It was almost like a picnic every time we went there to work together. Mama would pack a lunch and we would fix up a nice place where the babies could be comfortable.

There was a very nice swimming hole in the irrigation canal that was just the right depth for the kids to play in. This was something we all enjoyed doing. We could combine work and play here.

As soon as the beans started to bloom, I figured that we needed some bees to pollinate them. I had picked up a hive or two from here and there, but it was not enough. I happened to read in the *Stockton Record* newspaper where there were some bees for sale. I answered the ad and arranged to meet the owners in Farmington where they had their bees.

They were Miles Ponton and Johnny Clemons. They were partners in the bees business and their bees had grown in numbers to the point where they couldn't take care of them and work for the phone company, too. They were wanting to sell off about half of them for ten dollars a three decker colony.

I took Jim and Jerry with me and we met them at the given time and place. We looked the bees over and decided that we could not buy all that they wanted to sell. All we wanted was ten hives or so. We talked for some time and we made a deal with them to work their bees for them. They were down in the Oakdale and Farmington area in the star thistle and clover. On the week ends we would all go out and work the bees and take the honey off.

In the meantime, I was collecting swarms wherever I could find them till we had some twenty-five hives or so. We put them in with Miles and Johnny's bees when they put them in the almonds for pollination. We'd get a dollar for each hive.

We kept this arrangement for several years till the two of them were a-goin' out of the bee business all together. Miles sold all of his share, but Johnny kept his and had me and Jim and Jerry work them for him.

One day he said, "Walt, I want to sell you my bees and as soon as you get the money you can pay me for them."

I figured that this would be the year that they would do good and I could pay him for them. But it seemed that there was a big hole for that money and the bees didn't do all that good. I didn't have enough to give him any at all. I felt bad about it, so every time I would butcher a beef or a pig, I would give him a half or a quarter, so I kinda figured that would be the interest on what I owed him on the bees.

We were in the bee business now. That was something I had wanted to do all of my life. We didn't have enough to make a living on, but they did help feed the family.

It seemed that we were always a-movin' bees, into the almonds or the cherries or the clover for pollination. This is where we made most of our money. In fact, we made more off the pollination than we did off the honey.

I kept bees for the next forty years, but never could make enough from them to make the switch over to relying on them entirely for our livelihood.

Getting back to the Kentucky Wonder Beans: The beans grew well without too much effort on our part and we had a happy family time working together.

Then, when we were in the middle of harvesting the beans we discovered that I was pregnant again. I couldn't believe it because I felt so well. I had been very sick during the last two pregnancies. This baby would be due about the middle of February 1953.

But now we had another problem. We really didn't have the money for me to go to the doctor, so we decided that I would go to the county hospital. We were considered "indigent" because we didn't have any money and Daddy wasn't able to work much. We were thankful that there was some place for me to go. It cost me one dollar for each trip that I made.

We were bringing in a little money with the sale of honey from our bees. We had a jar sitting up on the fireplace mantel. We called it "the honey money jar". There were a lot of times when it made a big difference to the welfare of our family. We were just barely getting by.

We had been a-strugglin' to made ends meet, getting a little plaster job here and there,and bringing in a little money from the bees. It was early fall by now and Mama was pregnant again.

Then there came an opening for a mason at the Stockton State Hospital, a mental institution, and I got the job! This job consisted of doing maintainance in all of the "mud" trades such as plastering, cement finishing, tile setting, brick laying, and all emergency repairs of that nature. It paid three hundred dollars a month. That wasn't much, but it would be steady work and I figured I could make up the difference in what we needed some how. Anyway, it was better than I'd been a-doin'.

I was given a shop and a little office and a flatbed truck to drive to haul all of my stuff around in. I will never forget the first day that I spent on the job. I was setting a tile shower and I was having an awful hard time of it. The level that I was using was out of plumb and the shower looked like it.

At the end of the day when I looked at it, I was not happy with it. So I took it all down, washed off all of the tile, scraped off the wall, and hauled out all of the mess that I had made. By that time it was long after five o'clock and everybody had gone home. At least my immediate boss was gone and that was what was important to me. I could not fail 'cause I needed this job to feed all of my kids.

The next day was Saturday and that was a non-work day for

everybody except the technicians. So I decided that I would go buy a good level and try it again on Saturday and Sunday when there was no danger of the boss a-comin' in and seeing that I was not a very good tile setter.

Well, I didn't have so much trouble this time. In fact, it didn't look too bad at all. I finished it up late Sunday evening and polished it all off, doing everything that I could do to make it look as good as I could.

When the boss, Louie, saw it on Monday morning he was surprised and well pleased. However, I didn't tell him that I had worked over the weekend to make it look that way. I thought that I had covered up my tracks pretty well. But not well enough!

He saw through them and said, "Walter, I didn't expect you to work all weekend to finish this up. We were not in that big of a hurry for it, but being as you did, we'll pay you time and a half for the two days you worked. But next time, let me know if you are going to work on the weekend."

I guess I had worked there for over a month before they gave me any patients to help me. In some ways this made my work easier, but now I had to herd patients around, too. Work was considered good therapy for them.

In the morning I would go to the office and pick up my orders and then go over to the cottages to pick up the patients that I had to work that day. Sometimes there were so many patients that I had a hard time hauling them all on the truck. It bothered me to not get out as much work as I thought that I should when I had to spend so much of my time with the patients.

I could tell you a lot of interesting tales about this, but I'll save that for another time, in another book.

I worked there for eight years till I had some medical problems because of so much stress and I had to quit.

Chapter Thirty-seven

BABY LINDA

I had been a-workin' at the Stockton State Hospital, for several months. On this particular day I was setting tile in the bathroom for one of the doctors that worked there. It was about two o'clock in the afternoon on February 9, 1953 when Louie, my boss, came in there where I was a-workin'. He was excited, so much so that he could hardly talk.

Well, after he was through talking, this is what it was. Mama had gone out to the County Hospital at French Camp to have number eight, our last little baby. And that was Linda Lee. I had gone through it a few times before and I was not nearly as excited as Louie was. He didn't having any kids. He insisted that I drop everything that I was a-doin' and go to the hospital immediately.

Well, I felt that it was a pretty good excuse to leave work, so I got in our yellow flat-bed pickup and headed for the hospital. By the time that I had gotten there, the little one had just arrived, and as I walked in, there was a nurse a carrying her out to clean her up. She held her up for me to see. She was as pretty as a picture and I wanted to hold her, but they wouldn't let me.

It was not too long after that that we brought her home and there was a lot of excitement among the rest of the seven kids at home. I thought that they would love her to pieces and I had to have my turn, too.

I think that it was fourteen days later when I got home from work that I noticed that she was a-breathin' different than the rest of the little babies had.

I said, "Mama, how long has she been a-breathin' this way?"

"Almost all of the day. I think she has a cold and it's hard for her to breathe." she answered.

I said, "Well, I have to go up to Valley Springs to see about the cows up there that we have on pasture. Get your coat and the

153

baby and come with me."

It was some twenty-five miles up there and it was a nice drive. I thought some fresh air would do her good. So Mama got her coat and the baby and we started out for the hills.

I had to stop at Waterloo to get some gas, and when I killed the motor, I had a hard time a-gettin' it started again.

Then Mama said, "Daddy, I think we had better not go this time." We finally got the car started and went back home.

I held the baby for a while and Mama fried some potatoes for supper and we all sat down and ate.

After supper, I was holding the baby. She didn't look just right. So I said to Mama, "I think that we had better take her to the doctor."

We decided that we'd better take her back out to the County Hospital at French Camp where she was born. So we called Mom to come and take care of the other kids, and headed for the hospital.

At the hospital emergency room there was a long line of people standing there to be waited on. So we got in line and stood there a-waitin' for our turn. I figured that it would be at least a half hour or so. I guess that there were at least fifteen people ahead of us a-waitin' to see the doctor for one thing or another.

A young doctor walked in the room where we were a-waitin' in line. He looked our way and then he looked again. The second time he was a-lookin' right at the baby. Then he raised his head as high as he could as if to see over the rest of the heads of the people a-waitin' there in line.

Pointing to me, he said, "Bring the baby up here."

He had to tell me a couple of time to get me to understand what he wanted. So we went to where he was standing and I was a-saying that there were a lot of other people ahead of me. You know, he never paid a bit attention to me. He started giving orders to the nurses to drop everything they were a-doin'.

He said, "We have an emergency on our hands."

Boy, I mean, they got in high gear to get that baby some oxygen. As soon as things settled down a little, I asked the doctor if she was a-goin' to be okay.

All he said was, "I'll do the best that I can for her and that is all I can tell you."

Well, baby Linda Lee was in an oxygen tent for four days and stayed there for a couple more days before she was able to come home.

They said she had tracheal bronchitis and that she might have trouble a-breathin' when she caught a cold and they told us to watch her real close when she did.

Linda was just fourteen days old. All day long I hovered over her, watching and wondering. She wasn't breathing right. None of the other babies had had this problem and I didn't know what to do. I didn't have a car and Daddy was at work where it was a little difficult to reach him.

So I waited until he got home. We both looked at her and still wondered and worried about her but decided we'd watch and wait a little more.

Daddy has told you about our deciding not to go check on the cows. He says that he noticed that her fingernails were getting blue, but I don't remember being aware of that until we got her to the hospital and the nurse brought it to our attention.

It didn't take the doctors and nurses long to get her into an oxygen tent. Then we had to leave her there and go home. That was a very empty feeling to carry that brand new baby blanket home without our baby in it.

Daddy's brother, Henry, and his wife had lost a baby from whooping cough and pneumonia at that same hospital just six or seven months previous to Linda's trouble and they were all sure we'd lose her, too.

At the County Hospital they had some very strict rules about parents coming to visit their children. There were very few visiting hours and you couldn't go just any day you wanted to. Even talking to the nurses about the children was difficult. Parents just didn't have any rights at all. So just about all we could do was wait and pray.

I had been nursing the baby and as I waited to bring her back home, I tried to keep my milk up for her by pumping my breasts. I knew she needed that good mama milk. I was uncomfortable for a couple of days, but with the work of caring for seven other children, which included a set of fourteen month old twins, and worrying about the baby, in just a few days, my milk was all gone. There was none left for baby Linda. I'd have to give her a bottle.

155

A week later, they called from the hospital and told us we could bring her home. That was one of the most welcome telephone calls I ever received in my life. I didn't like having an empty baby blanket. When Daddy and I walked in with our baby Linda back in her blanket, all the other kids cheered and shouted for joy.

The doctor gave me instructions to keep a vaporizer in her room. With eight kids, she didn't have her own room. In fact, we had three cribs in our bedroom. A vaporizer wouldn't have done her much good in there and we didn't have the money to buy one, anyway.

So for the next month or two, every time she would get croupy I'd wrap her up in a blanket and take her into the "little" bathroom and turn on the hot water in the shower. Sometimes we'd stay in there for one or two hours, until she was breathing easier and able to sleep. For the next few months, I hovered over her and watched her every time she got a cold. And with seven other kids in the family it seemed that someone had a cold all the time.

One time when I took her to the well baby clinic and explained about her problem, they told me that she would probably get the croup easily until she was six years old. But she didn't. That was the only time she ever had any problems with it. We were thankful for that.

Mama with Linda when she was 2½ months old.

Chapter Thirty-eight

ROCK A BYE BABIES AND LULLABIES

Allen was four years old when Johnny and Merri Lou were born. He was my <u>big</u> helper boy. He'd go get diapers, bottles, and whatever I needed whenever I needed it. I guess he must have saved me a million steps and tons of energy.

He had a little rocking chair that someone had given him for Christmas. He would sit in it and visit with me while I was rocking Johnny and Merri Lou. When they got big enough, and that didn't take very long, I would let him hold and rock one of them while I rocked the other one. When Linda came along, he would rock one of them, while I rocked the other two.

Allen and I had those babies so spoiled that they wouldn't go to sleep unless they were rocked. I guess I liked to rock them because that gave me a chance to rest for a while as well as cuddle them. They were all toddlers before they would go to sleep without being rocked.

Daddy had been working very hard on his job and was a little stressed out. He was having a hard time getting all the rest and sleep he needed to be able to work each day, so we took the three baby cribs out of our bedroom and created a nursery in the smallest bedroom downstairs. That worked very well, and Daddy was able to get more rest.

One night, one of the babies woke up and began to cry, so I got up to take care of it. Before I was done changing that diaper, the other two babies woke up and had to be changed, too. I gave each of them a bottle and tucked them in, then went back to bed. But those bottles didn't last very long and they were all crying again in a few minutes.

I got up and put the twins, who were about eighteen months old, in the rocking chair. I went back and picked up Linda, who was about four months old. Some how I managed to get into the rocking chair with all three babies in my lap. Then I rocked them until they all went back to sleep.

I had each of them wrapped up warmly, but I was getting cold, at least my feet were cold. It must have been between one and two in the morning. Everyone was asleep but me. I didn't know how I was going to get those babies back to bed, so I continued to rock them for a while until I could figure out just what I could do. I sure didn't want to wake Daddy up.

Finally, I very carefully slipped out from under them, leaving one of the twins on the rocking chair. I carried the other twin and the little one to their beds, putting down the little one first. Then I went back and picked up the twin that I had left on the rocking chair.

I succeeded! They all stayed asleep!

Rocking babies was a very important activity in our family. They all liked to be rocked, even when they were almost too big to put on my lap.

Linda, especially, liked to be rocked. Someone took a picture of her asleep on my lap when she was about six years old. She didn't like that picture when she was a child. I think she felt that people would think she was really a baby if they saw that picture. Whenever we introduced our children to someone, we introduced her as our baby. She didn't like that, either. Now that she has children of her own, she likes to be called our baby. She sent me a birthday card one year with a cartoon picture of a great big baby and a very small mother on it. The caption said, "Happy Birthday Mother from your Baby."

One of the kids' favorite things for Daddy to do was for him to sing to them when they were little. He always said that he could only sing tenor – ten or eleven times worse than anybody else. But they didn't care about the quality. It was the loving attention they were getting. Their attention span expanded when he sang to them and they enjoyed it very much. And his songs could always soothe a tear stained face and bring a smile.

Burl Ives was Daddy's favorite singer. We had several of his records. Daddy learned to sing many of the songs just from listening to the records. He sang "A Froggy Went A-courtin'" with so many verses that at the end, he would sing, "If you want any more you can sing it yourself." They always got a big kick out of that.

He would also sing "I Bought Me A Hen And My Hen Pleased

Me". That wasn't the name of it, but that was the first line, anyway. And he sang "My Bonnie Lies Over the Ocean", "Long, Long Ago", "Clementine", and others. One of them started out with these words, "When I was a little baby, I remember long ago, Mammy would sit all evening, and sing this song to me." These songs were for fun and excitement. Just yesterday, our son, Jerry called me for Mother's Day and was telling me that he sings these same songs that he learned as a child, to his grandson now.

I was the one who sang the lullabies for quiet time, rocking, and going to sleep. Sometimes it was a little hard to do with two babies (or even three when Johnny, Merri Lou and Linda were little.) Johnny got one about "my handsome, winsome Johnny". Merri Lou got, "Mary Lou, I Love You". Linda had her own special one, too, but I don't remember the name of it now. She got a lot of "special attention" after all of the others were in school. Of course, they all got "Rock-a-bye Baby". These were wonderful, close, quiet times that we all loved.

It's been too long ago for me to remember what I sang to the older ones when they were little. But we had some favorite story books that got read over and over for many years. As I read them, the kids memorized them. If I didn't read them right, the kids would correct me. These were some of the most precious moments with my children.

Years and years and years later, as I was sorting through the pictures for this book, I became sad because all my "babies" were gone. Even as I am writing this, there are tears in my eyes. I am sure there are a lot of you mothers who understand this.

Linda at six months.

Merri Lou, Johnny, and Linda
in the late fall of 1953

Chapter Thirty-nine

JOHNNY'S FALL
MEDICINE FOR MERRI LOU

One day me 'n Mama were a-sittin' at the table trying to stretch out my paycheck to cover all of the bills that we had and still have some money left over to buy some groceries, too.

On this particular day, I had gone down to the box factory and had gotten a load of blocks to burn in the fireplace to keep the house warm 'cause that was all of the heat we had in the house.

Johnny was a-playin' with some of the blocks. I guess that he was not yet two years old. He picked up this little block that was about three quarters of an inch square and about ten or eleven inches long. It was broken off where there was a knot, and it left a sharp point on one end. Mama told him several times to keep it out of his mouth. Me 'n Mama were both so involved in our bill paying that we didn't pay close enough attention to him.

The next thing we knew Johnny had fallen out the back door with this stick in his mouth and had landed on it. He was making a gurgling sound as he was a-cryin' and he was a-bleedin' from his mouth real bad. It made both of us scared. This happened about eleven o'clock in the morning.

I picked him up and we headed for the doctor who had taken out my appendix 'cause I knew he was a good one. His office was about ten miles from home and in the middle of town. When he looked at him he knew that he couldn't fix Johnny's problem at his office. He had torn his soft palate so that it was a-floppin' toward the front of his mouth. The doctor advised us to take him out to the San Joaquin County Hospital Emergency where it wouldn't cost us so much money.

By this time the bleeding had stopped and Johnny wasn't crying. So we headed for the County Hospital in French Camp, about twenty miles away. When we got there the people handling the patients couldn't see that we had any great emergency, so we had to wait what seemed a long time to us.

When the doctor there finally looked at Johnny, he told us that he'd have to put him in the hospital to operate on him to fix it. So we had to leave him there.

We registered him into the hospital and they took him away from us about five o'clock. They would do the surgery that evening and they wouldn't let us see him until the next day.

A couple of days later they called us and told us we could take him home, and we rushed over to the hospital to get him. When we looked in on him, he had a diaper and a little hospital gown on. He was with several other little kids in a play room. They had all been given a chocolate cupcake to eat.

Poor little Johnny couldn't eat because his mouth was so sore. All he could do was drink and that wasn't easy for him, either. I guess he thought he could, though, 'cause he had traded a toy for each of the other little kid's cupcakes. He had a stack of them all for himself on a little table. He looked up at us and offered us a cupcake.

We picked him up and took him home, thankful that his fall hadn't hurt him worse than it did. It was another week of two before he could eat and swallow very well.

To this day, he has a scar in the roof of his mouth. It still scares us when we think back on this event and what could have happened and didn't. Now every time we see a small child with a sharp pencil, pen, or stick we get scared all over again. We've never been able to keep our mouths shut. We always have to tell the mother about what happened to our little Johnny. We sure wouldn't want that to happen to any other little kid.

MEDICINE FOR MERRI LOU

One evening when I had come home from work, Mama told me that she and Valida, my sister-in-law, had been a-talkin'. Valida had just bought a new car and she wanted to take a little vacation trip. She wanted Mama to go along with her for the fun of it, and to help with the driving.

After supper we talked it over and I thought it was a good

idea. It would give Mama a little rest. She said that she would take the youngest child, Linda, with her. Linda was not quite two years old. It was between Christmas and New Year's Day and all the kids were home from school. The bigger kids could pretty well take care of themselves and the younger twins while I was at work. Mama would only be gone for two or three days and she could call home to see how things were going here. Besides she deserved and needed a little vacation. So they left early the next morning.

Well, everyone pitched in and really shined up the house and the girls did the laundry. We wanted everything in tip-top shape so that when Mama came home there would be nothing for her to do for a few days.

When she called home, she said that they were at the Grand Canyon and wanted to go down to Bisbee to visit the old homestead and Hazel, my sister, and they would be gone for a few more days than they had planned. This was quite a disappointment to all of us, but I didn't let on. We all wanted her to have a good time.

The next day, Merri Lou came down with something. She was real sick, throwing up and running a temperature. She was sicker than I thought she should be for anything that she would get over by herself, so I took her to see the doctor. He gave me some medicine in a bottle to give her every four hours till she got better.

I was working on a job that I had to be there every day. Oh, how I wished that Mama was home. She could make things all better right away. I felt the responsibility of a father and a mother, but I did the best that I could. The big girls were doing their best to keep things under control, but it was a hard job for them, too.

Everytime that Merri Lou would take this medicine, it would not stay down long enough to do her any good. In desperation, I told her if she would hold it down, I would buy her a doll. So, bless her heart, she did it. And she started getting better fast.

By the time that Mama got home the house was back to normal – it did not shine any more. We were one mighty happy family to see our Mama back home again. There is nobody who can take her place.

One day Charlotte thought she would play a joke on Merri Lou. Before it was time to go to bed, Charlotte hid under Merri

Lou's bed and laid there very quietly for a long time before the little kids went to bed. After everyone went to bed and the lights were all out, Charlotte began pushing up the mattress, which was a very thin one on link springs. This scared the dickens out of Merri Lou and she came out of that bed in a hurry.

She ran into our bedroom a-screamin' at the top of her voice, "Mama! Mama! There's a bum under my bed!"

Then here came Charlotte a-laughin' right behind her. She thought it was funny, but Merri Lou didn't. Merri Lou had a hard time being nice to Charlotte for the next few days, and Charlotte felt real bad 'cause she had done something to her sister that had made her feel bad.

Now they can laugh about it, but they sure didn't then.

Johnny, Merri Lou, and Linda

Chapter Forty

JIM'S LEG OPERATION

If you remember, early in our story we told you about Jim having only four toes on his right foot. When he was a little over two years old, I took him to see the doctor about it. His right knee would touch his left leg when he walked. We didn't know if anything could be done about it. After taking some x-rays and looking at Jim's leg, the doctor advised us to just leave him be until he was nearly grown. Then I should take him back for another look at it.

The summer he was twelve, 1953, I did take him back to see the doctor at the County Hospital and they did another evaluation of his leg situation.

This time the doctor strongly advised us to have surgery on his leg. He said he would take a piece of bone from his pelvic bone and put it into his leg just above the knee joint. That would straighten his leg and, hopefully, would stimulate growth in that leg.

I asked the doctor what his situation would be after the surgery. He said that he would have a full leg cast on and I probably could take him home after ten days.

I asked him what his fee would be. He said not to worry, they would work it out. Since we were having so many financial difficulties he told me that the county had a cripple children's fund that would take care of it for us. For that we were very thankful.

The surgery was scheduled for the first week in September, not at the County Hospital which was at French Camp, but at St. Joseph's Hospital which was in Stockton.

When I took him to the hospital they weighed him in at one hundred sixty-five pounds so they decided to put him in a men's ward instead of the children's ward.

I waited at the hospital during the surgery, and it seemed to take forever. When they finally brought him out, I expected to see his leg in a cast. I was shocked to find that he had a body cast from just above

165

his waistline to his toes on his right leg and to his knee on his left leg. But he had come through the surgery just fine.

Later that day, I learned that he would be in the hospital for a month or two. I wouldn't be able to take care of him at home, after all. He was going to miss a lot of school. After inquiring, I learned that we could get a county paid "home" teacher to come to the hospital three days a week so he wouldn't miss out on his schooling.

I arranged for this and we all settled down to the routine of our new situation with Jim. It didn't seem to bother him at all and he was a very good patient and also a good student.

I went to see him every day and Daddy would go whenever he could. I also took the other kids up to see him as often as I could. The hospital had a "no children under twelve" rule so I had to sneak them up the back stairs to take them in to see Jim. The nurses on the floor didn't care because they knew it was good for Jim's morale to see them. Of course, Jerry could go whenever he wanted to. That helped, too. I missed only two or three days going up to see him the whole time he was in the hospital.

They had put a bar over the top of his bed that he could grab hold of to move himself a little. Linda says that she can remember swinging on Jim's bar. She was only eight months when he went into the hospital and nearly ten months old when he came home.

After two months in the body cast, they took it off and put a full leg cast on his right leg. He still had to stay in the hospital another month for that.

They took his leg cast off and let Jim come home the day before Thanksgiving that year of 1953 and that made that Thanksgiving day a very special one for all of us. Jim had been in the hospital nearly three months.

For the next six weeks he walked with crutches. He got so he could swing along almost as fast as Jerry could run. He played football in the eighth grade and all through high school without his leg giving him too much trouble. His surgery did straighten his leg, but it never caught up with the other one in length. When he reached his full stature, he had to have his shoe built up to be comfortable when walking or standing. Some people thought of his leg as a handicap, but we never thought of it that way. As far as we were concerned he was a normal child.

Chapter Forty-one

THE PRETTY LITTLE HEIFER

One year we had decided to raise up a bunch of white leghorn fryers for the freezer. There was a feed store on East Main Street that we bought feed from for all of the live stock. They had a special on white leghorn baby chickens. In fact, they would give them to you if you bought all of your feed from them. This sounded like a good deal so we brought home a couple hundred of them to raise. We would go once a week to buy feed.

One day, when we went there to get feed, we saw a pretty little Holstein heifer calf in a pen all by herself. She was a registered heifer, or, I should say, just half of it was on her father's side. He was one of the top ten bulls of the nation at that time, called Neptune. To get some of this bulls semen cost a big pile of money, like fifty dollars. It was the early days of artificial insemination.

At the time this little heifer showed all of the potentials of making a real good milk cow. She was fed on a bottle of some kind of calf suckle, or something that was supposed to be the best thing that you could feed a calf. It was advertised as the next best thing to cows milk that you could feed a calf.

Every time we would go in there, Jim and Jerry would go over and pet her.

Well, one day when we were in the feed store, Jerry said to Jim, "Why don't we guess how much she weighs and see if we can win her?" So they both put down the same weight.

I said, "Why don't you both put down different weights? That way you would have a better chance of guessing the right weight."

But they both said no 'cause that is what they both thought she weighed. They were in the 4-H at the time and they figured that this heifer would make a good 4-H project. The date was posted when the winner of the calf would be announced.

On that day I had come home from plastering all day and we had had to work a little late to finish up the job. As soon as I got home, here were all of the kids a-waitin' for me in the drive way.

Jim and Jerry said, "Daddy, today is when the drawing is at the feed store and if we aren't there we will miss out. Maybe we could be the winners. Maybe if we go right now, maybe we can make it before it closes."

So all of the bigger kids piled in the car and away we all went.

We were about a block away from the feed store when one of the kids said, "Daddy, there is a cop with his red light on that wants to pass you!"

But I waited till I got to the feed store to pull over and he pulled in right behind me. I knew what I had done. I was a-goin' too fast and he was about to give me a ticket.

He asked me for my driver's license and I reached for it. It wasn't in my pocket! I told him I must have lost it at work or maybe I had left it home when I changed from my plastering work clothes in a hurry so I could take the kids to the feed store before it closed, 'cause they were going to announce the winner of the calf at closing time. Anyway, I didn't have it.

He asked, "Where have you been plastering?" and I told him the address.

Then a smile came over his face and he said, "Why, that's where my mother lives and she thinks you're <u>all right</u>!"

Then he said, "You know that it is not a good idea to go too fast when you have a whole car full of kids for two reasons. One is that you're teaching them bad habits by not obeying the law, and the other is you might get into a wreck and hurt them."

By now, everybody was a-lookin' out the windows of the feed store at us and the cop said, "Well, let's go in and see who won this heifer you are talking about."

I was off the hook, but I still didn't know what had happened to my wallet.

As soon as we got into the feed store, the owner got out all of the names of the people who had guessed how much the heifer weighed. Low and behold, Jim and Jerry were the winners!

As the cop went out the door he said to me, "Go down tomorrow and get yourself a new driver's license and be careful and don't do any more speeding."

Well, the next day we borrowed the neighbor's cow trailer and took the new heifer home. The feed store man came out with his camera and took some pictures of the two boys and that heifer and put it up in his feed store so people could see who were the lucky ones.

She was as pretty a little heifer as I had ever seen. She looked like she would grow into a good milk cow. Things were going along pretty good and the heifer was doing real well.

One day I stayed home from work 'cause I was a little under the weather with a cold. I had gone out to gather the eggs when I heard Johnny screaming. I ran over to see what was the matter with him, and here was this pretty little heifer after him. She almost got him before he was able to make it under the fence.

Now this was not the first time she had done this. Jim and Jerry had complained to me that she had a mean streak in her, but I passed it off as not being anything too serious. If it was a bull acting that way, I would have done something about it immediately. Just a couple of days before, one of the neighbors that had a little dairy just up the road from us was killed by a Holstein bull, and he wasn't very big, either. That bull was about the same age as the boys pretty little heifer.

I got to thinking about this and the more that I thought about it the madder I got. I could visualize this heifer a-hurtin' one of the kids. So as bad as I was a-feein' with my cold, I hooked up the cow trailer and proceeded to load up this pretty little heifer. Some how she didn't look so pretty any more to me. She looked more like T-bone steaks and hamburgers in our freezer. And that is just what happened to her. She went to Orvis and Clinger's slaughter house.

But that's not end of this story. I guess it was a couple of weeks later that here came the feed man out to see to see that pretty little heifer. He had brought some other people with him to show them how well she had done on the kind of feed that he was a-sellin'.

I had to be honest so I told him what had happened. He was very upset, to say the least, but not nearly as upset as I would have been if that pretty little heifer had hurt or killed one of my little kids. But after about two years he got over it and saw it my way.

Jerry and Jim with the Pretty Little Heifer

Chapter Forty-two

MOVING BEES

It was back in the fifties. I had just finished eating supper after a hard day of plastering. I had just settled down to reading the paper when the phone rang. It was Johnny Clemons on the other end asking if I would help him move a couple of loads of bees out of the cherry orchards in Linden and take them down to Oakdale, some twenty-five miles away, to put them in the Ladino clover for pollination. He was a-gettin' something like two dollars a hive for all of the time that they were there and that was a lot of money to get all in one bunch.

Well, I told him I would as soon as I went in and took a shower and washed a little plaster off of me. He was to pick me up in about an hour. I would much rather have gone to bed, I was so tired, but Johnny was a good old boy and would do anything in the world for me at any time and here was my turn to help him.

We pulled into the orchard and there was a truck a-sittin' there all ready to go and another one was about half loaded. You see, his partner, Miles Ponton, was a-helpin' him, but he had gotten real sick and Johnny had taken him home.

We finished loading and tied both loads down and were ready to go by about nine in the evening. Then we started out for Oakdale. I dreaded it in the worst way. I was so sleepy and tired I wasn't too sure I could drive the twenty-five miles to Oakdale.

I rolled down the windows and let the cold breeze blow on me. I was about half frozen in about ten miles, but I figured it was better to be frozen than go to sleep a-drivin'. The cold air would keep me awake.

We had gone what seemed to me a long, long way down the road, when all of a sudden I woke up and the truck I was a-drivin' was having a hard time of staying on all four of its wheels. That truck waited till it had passed a big irrigation ditch before it decided to run off the road and stop. I was lucky!

Well, I got out and looked the load all over and all of the bees were still tied down pretty good. I hadn't lost any of them. I boxed the load a little, but nothing serious.

By then Johnny had turned around and was back there where I was. I was a-shakin', but I do believe that he was more scared than I was.

He said, "Are you all right, Walt? Can you go on now? It's only a couple of miles down the road to the right where we will unload them."

I said, "Sure, I am too scared to go to sleep now. Besides I'm about half frozen, too."

Well, I went down the road about a mile and that dumb truck went off the road again, but I was able to get it up and back on the road before Johnny had time to turn around and come back. After much difficulty I finally got that truck load of bees to where they were supposed to go.

I soon woke up when those mean bees started a-stingin' me when we started to unload them. I guess we were most of the night unloading them. There were some two hundred or so hives.

Well, I made it back home after about three naps along the side of the road. I fell into bed and the rest of the night I slept double-time.

I didn't feel too bad at work the next day or even all the rest of the week, for that matter.

It was the next Friday night when I got another phone call from Johnny. He had the flu real bad and Miles was still sick.

He said, "Walt, I hate to ask you to do this, but those bees need to be worked or they will all be a-swarmin'. Will you go out there and work as many as you can till I get to feeling a little better?"

I said, "Sure." After all, when a friend is in trouble you gotta help him.

So the next morning I took Jim and Jerry and took along enough lunch for an army and we headed out to the bee yard to do what we could. I knew that we could not get over them all, but we would do what we could. Having the two boys to do a lot of the running for me helped a lot.

We lit up the bee smoker and buttoned up our clothes the best that we could. We didn't have any bee gloves. Our hands and wrists were bare. At first we were a'doin' fine till those bees started a-stingin' us on the hands and wrists.

I do believe that each one of the boys was trying to out last the other one, and I was a-takin' a few stings myself. I thought, if those two boys can stand it, I sure could.

Well, we got through most of them, but I started a-feelin' sorry for those boys.

I said, "Let's quit for the day." And they were ready to quit.

The next day their hands and wrists were swollen up so bad that they couldn't close their hands and they had to stay home from school.

Those boys were a-learnin' to be beekeepers real fast. I was real proud of them. They were never quitters no matter how hard it was or how many times they got stung.

Walter with a swarm of bees

Walter, Jerry, and Jim with
a load of new honey.

Our honey business

Chapter Forty-three

ELSIE

One warm day in the summer we decided to make ice cream. The closest place to get ice was a little country store about two miles away on Linden Road at a fruit worker's camp which was in an orchard. Daddy went to get the ice. I had the ice cream all mixed up and waiting in the freezer. The kids were anxious to get going with it.

Daddy should have been back home in less than a half hour, but he wasn't. After an hour of waiting we decided that he must have got to talking with someone, which he often does. Then, after almost two hours of waiting, we were beginning to really get worried.

I was just about to send one of the boys to see if he could find him, when he slowly drove in with a woman carrying a baby and two or three other kids. The car was loaded with boxes of her things.

We were all curious about what was taking place so we gathered around to find out what it was. Daddy introduced Elsie and her kids and told us that they would all be staying with us for a few days.

I thought, Whoa! Let's wait a minute here. I'm not just too sure about this. But I decided to keep my mouth shut and listen.

Daddy explained that Elsie's husband had abandoned her and the children, leaving her with no money and the cabin rent was due. She was in the little store when Daddy went in to buy the ice, and the camp manager had just told her that she would have to move out.

Now Daddy is one of the most caring and compassionate men that I know and his first instinct was to tell her that she and her children could come to live with us for a few days while she located her husband. She hadn't lived in the state long enough to get any state help and had no one to turn to.

Daddy told her that she would have to work with me and do her part of helping me keep up the housework to pay for her keep. She didn't hesitate to take up his offer. Now here she was and we had to make arrangements for them in our family.

We moved the girls out of the bigger back bedroom and put them in the smaller bedroom. With all of us cooperating it didn't take us long to get Elsie and her children comfortable.

Elsie did what she said she would and we all got along fine. She helped me cook and keep up the house and it really wasn't too much of an inconvenience for us. But the few days turned into a few weeks when Elsie couldn't locate her husband.

She had been with us for about six weeks, when one day her husband just showed up. He still didn't have any prospects for work, but we welcomed him to come in to stay over night with his family. The next day he looked for work, and the next, and the next, and the next, but he didn't find any.

In the meantime, with her husband "home", Elsie wouldn't do any more work in the house to help me. She preferred to be with her husband. Their kids started to misbehave under their father's influence, but they all still expected to be fed. Wow! What more could one expect? A free roof over your head and all you wanted to eat and no bills to worry about, what could be better than that?

Now this was an intolerable situation for us. Our own kids were getting very unhappy about it and everyone seemed to be angry with everybody else. Daddy and I talked together and decided they would have to go. So we talked to them and told them that we couldn't keep them with us any longer.

Daddy went to the auto parts store and bought a roof-top carrier for their car and gave them enough money for gas and food for a couple of days, then stayed home from work to make sure that they left.

They did leave, but they were so mad at us for asking them to leave that they never even said thank you or goodbye.

People are funny. When they are down and out and you feel compassion for them, they respond to kindness and behave well. But when you've done too much for them they turn against you and you become their enemy. They become just like the cow stuck in the mud in "me 'n Henry". You pull them out and they'll take out after you like it was all your fault that they got into the mud and you have to run for your life.

This is a lesson we've had to learn over and over and over again throughout our whole life.

Chapter Forty-four

BILL

Part of my job at the Stockton State Hospital was to take some of the mentally ill patients out with me to teach them some of these skills that I knew. There was no time limit on how fast the work got done, but whenever I got it done was okay. Sometimes, I could have done it myself in half of the time. The amount of men I had a-workin' with me varied from two to six or eight. It seemed that the more that I had, the longer it took to get the work done.

I had to go to the cottages where they were a-livin', unlock the door, and take them out with me. Then I'd bring them back in the afternoon when we were through working. This was done to keep them from wandering off. It was not that they were bad and mean or anything like that. That is, most of the time. If they got mean I just left them locked up in the cottage where they lived.

I guess that when you have that many men a-workin' with you all of the time, there are some favorites. Some of them just responded better and worked a little better.

Well, this was the way with Bill Harris, a big black man in his late forties. I could always depend on him. He was neat and clean and was always there to help me. He never talked very much, but would periodically laugh out loud. When you would ask him what he was a-laughin' at he would most usually say, "I thought of something funny." But he would never tell me what it was that he was a-thinkin' about.

One day he was in a talkative mood. We were pouring a side-walk and while we were a-waitin' for the cement to set up so that we could trowel it we were a-sittin' in a couple of wheel barrows. He started telling me about his life as a young man.

He said, "I had eight brothers and sisters and I was in the middle somewhere. My Mama and Papa lived in South Carolina on the edge of town. My Papa worked at whatever he could get to feed us kids and my Mama washed other peoples clothes and did ironing. We lived mostly on cornbread and sow belly.

"When we were rich, that is, when Papa would get paid 'till all of the money was all gone, we would get some canned salmon and save the cans to drink out of.

"When I got a little older, I started to work in a brick yard a-stackin' bricks and you had to get 'em straight. If you didn't you got fired and someone else would get your job. It was a good job and I liked it. I got twenty-five cents a day and got paid once a month. And I was a-savin' up my money. I wanted to go to school and learn to be an engineer so I could go to Africa and help build railroads there.

"Every payday I would give my Mama two dollars for my keep and I would put the rest in a Mason jar and bury it in the chicken house so no one could find it. I did this for several years 'till I had a lot of money. I had two Mason jars full of money. By then I was twenty-one and figured that I had about enough money to go to college.

"One day I came home from work and my Papa was as drunk as a skunk. I decided it was time for me to leave home. I went out where I had my money buried and it was all gone. There wasn't any left there at all. All there was was empty Mason jars with the lids off a-layin' there in the chicken pen.

"I got mad 'cause all of my money was gone. I would never be able to build railroads in Africa.

"I don't know what happened after that except that one day I was in a grape vineyard in Fresno, California when a couple of cops came and got me and put me in jail. Then I don't remember nothin' till I was in this place.

"They used to beat me a lot, but now they don't any more. This is not a college, but it is something. I don't know what it really is. I have never figured it out. I sure wish I had some poke salad or some turnip greens. Even a little sow belly would sure taste good."

The sidewalk was ready to finish by then and when we got it all done, I took Bill back to his cottage and I went home.

Some time later, I got to thinking of this story that Bill told me. The more I thought about it, the more I felt like this was something that he would really like. We had a wood-burning stove in our shop at work where we kept all of the tools. So one day, when I went to work, I took along with me, a pot and some plates and some turnips out of the garden and a ham bone.

I said to Bill, "I want you to cook these turnips and we will eat them for lunch. You stay in the shop and do the cooking and before I come in for lunch, I will stop by the bakery and get us some bread. If they are making pies, I'll bring an apple pie." This brought a big smile over Bill's face.

The hospital bakery was run by a baker who had a lot of mental patients helping him just as I had patients helping me. It was the same in the kitchen. In fact, most all of the food that was used at the hospital was raised out at the State Hospital farm. They had cows for milk and pigs for pork.

Well, when I came in for lunch, Bill had a big pot of turnips with greens all ready to eat. He was a good cook. They were lip smackin' good!

Well, me 'n Bill got to be great friends and he kept a-sayin' how he would like to go back to his home in South Carolina, but he figured that all of his folks were gone by then. He would say from time to time that he would like to live on a farm. He'd keep talking to me about my place. It was not a farm like the one that he knew when he was a small boy.

One day I asked him if he would like to come and live on us on our little ten acre place. The more we talked about it, the more he wanted to do it. He could have the run of the place and help me from time to time. After a while he decided he'd like to do that.

So the boys and I built a little house just for him. It was just a little one room shack about ten by ten, with a wood stove in it. When everything was ready, he got permission to leave the hospital and come to stay with us.

He cooked most all of his meals except for dinner on Sunday. Then he would eat with us in the house. We always remembered his birthday with a family birthday party. Mama would make a cake for him and we'd all sing *Happy Birthday To You* for him.

He was real happy there. He would sit in the shade of a big walnut tree and entertain himself by figuring out how much material it would take to build a railroad ten miles long, from all of the ties, to all of the spikes to hold the rails down, to the track. He was just a good old black man that never hurt anybody.

Several years later, we were getting ready to make a move to

Arizona. I asked Bill if he wanted to come along with us. He said he was afraid of the snakes out in Arizona and wanted to go back to the hospital. So just before we left, he said goodbye to all of the family and I took him back to the Stockton State Hospital.

Well, from there, he was put in a boarding house with some other men from the same hospital. As the years went by, Jerry would go to see him. By then, Jerry was a deputy sheriff. One day he remembered that it was Bill's birthday, so he got him a little present and took it over to him.

Bill was really happy and he wanted a picture of himself and Jerry a-standin' together. So Jerry asked the landlady to take a picture of the two of them and he gave a copy of it to him. Bill kept it up on the dresser in his bed room where he could look at it, 'cause Jerry was the only family that he had.

By this time Bill was getting into his seventies. Every morning, he would take a mile walk before breakfast. One morning he did not come back so the landlady started a-lookin' for him. She called the sheriff and they found him dead over on California and Pine Streets.

When they went to his room to see if they could locate his next of kin so they could tell them about Bill, they couldn't find any. They saw Jerry's picture with Bill on the dresser and recognized him 'cause they worked with him. So they called Jerry and told him about what had happened. Jerry was the closest "next of kin" that Bill had. Jerry took over and saw to it that he was buried properly and he conducted the funeral.

Our whole family was saddened when we heard of the news of Bill's passing. He had been a good friend. We felt good that we were able to have known him and shared some of our lives with him.

Bill Harris

Chapter Forty-five

A GOOD NEIGHBOR &
FARMING OUR TEN ACRES

I guess that everybody, at some time or another, has a neighbor like Manuel Lyle. He was always there when there was a need. He lived up the road a little piece, about a quarter of a mile or so on the other side of the road in a big old-fashioned house that was built of redwood siding with a big porch on three sides of it. He made his living by milking a few cows and doing a little tomato farming in the summertime. He was just a down-right good neighbor.

He was always a-helpin' me and whenever he needed help a-bailin' hay, I would go over and help him. Whatever was needed, we helped each other.

Well, this particular time I will always remember. This was one of those times when the whole family was down with the flu. It was in the dead of winter and as cold as kraut outside. All we had to heat the house with was a couple of electric heaters and a fireplace. When we would run out of wood for the fireplace, we would turn on the wall heaters. Then the electric bill would go sky high. This was one of those mornings that everything that could go wrong did.

We heard a knock on the door. It was Mr. Lyle. He had come over to see what was the matter 'cause he hadn't seen us around for a couple of days. He didn't seem to mind that the house was full of sick people and he might catch what we had. He didn't ask if there was anything that he could do. He just went into the kitchen and got the milk bucket and went out to do the chores. He came back in the house with a bucket full of milk and said that the sow pig had had little ones during the night. She didn't make a nest for them and it looked as if they were all dead.

So he went out and gathered them all up and put them in an

apple box and brought them into the house where it was warm.

Mr. Lyle could see that we were in pretty bad shape and he was ready to help in any way that he could.

He said, "Why don't I go home and get my trailer and load up that sow pig and take her down to the auction sale this morning?" So I told him that would be a good idea if he didn't mind doing it.

By the time that he had gotten back with his cow trailer, those little pigs had come to life and were a-jumpin' all over the place. We all thought that they were all done for, 'cause they had gotten so cold. There were eight of them, all a'wantin' something to eat.

Well, Mr. Lyle didn't have any trouble loading up the sow, and her little pigs. He was gone till late in the afternoon. When he came back he had his cow trailer loaded to the top with wood. He had taken some of the money from the pigs and had gone by the box factory and picked up a load of pine block scraps for us.

He unloaded them and brought in a good supply to last the rest of the day and he gave me the rest of the money.

We built a big fire in the fireplace and we gathered all 'round to get good and warm. It seemed to make everything all better when we felt the warm fire and the warmth of a good friend.

It seemed that most of the time it was a real struggle to feed and clothe all of the kids. We did everything that we could think of to make ends meet and sometimes they didn't quite make it.

Our little ten acre place was nice rich farm land with plenty of well water. The farmers around there planted various crops from alfalfa to tomatoes. We thought that tomatoes would be a good crop for us to plant 'cause we had all of these kids to help pick the tomatoes. That year the cannery was paying a pretty good price for them. But the only trouble was, we didn't have anything to work the ground with but an old Fordson Model T tractor – and no plows or any other kind of tools that we needed.

Mr. Lyle had a team of horses, Molly and Belle. One was all white and the other one was a sort of red color. We hired him and his team of horses to work up the ground and get it ready to plant. In the meantime, he also helped me with the preparing of a hotbed for the tomato plants. He was a good farmer. That is all he did all of his life. I don't think that he ever did anything else. He was everybody's friend and good neighbor.

After we got all of the tomatoes planted, he would come over every so often and check on me to see if I was doing all of the things that I should be a-doin'. The biggest job was to keep the weeds out. It seemed to me that they grew faster than the tomatoes did. We would all hoe the tomatoes after work and school and on weekends. From the littlest to the biggest, everybody had a row to hoe. It was a game with the bigger ones to see who could get to the end of his row before the other one did so that he could help the littler kids finish his row. It was a lot of hard work, but it was a lot of fun, too.

As soon as the tomatoes started a-gettin' ripe we went down to the cannery and got a load of boxes to haul our tomatoes in to the cannery. I don't know whether our backs ached worse when we hoed the weeds or picked the tomatoes.

Well, the tomatoes looked real good and it looked like there would be a good crop – no bugs and no blight. Everything really looked good. Me and Mama talked it over and we decided to get a new Ford tractor and a plow and a disk so that next year we could work the ground ourselves without hiring so much of it done.

The day that they brought the tractor out was a real big thing. As soon as it was unloaded in the front yard everybody wanted to drive it, but mostly, Jim and Jerry. We used it to pull a four wheeled trailer to gather the tomatoes out of the field after they were in the boxes.

One day, Allen, who was four years old, came up to me and put his hand on top of his head and measured himself to my leg as he said, "Daddy, I am big now. Huh, Daddy?"

I said, "You sure are Allen, and getting bigger all of the time."

"I am big enough to drive the tractor, huh, Daddy?"

Now, who could say no to a little boy that wanted so much to drive the tractor.

So I said, "Sure, You can sit on my lap and I will help you."

He said, "No. I am big enough. I can do it all by myself."

Then I said, "Well, okay, but watch out for the boxes of tomatoes and don't run over them."

"I know," he said, "**I know!**"

So I put the tractor in the lowest gear that it would go and stood back and let him drive it all by himself, warning him of the boxes of tomatoes just ahead.

Then he went right ahead and ran over one of the boxes of

tomatoes and squashed them all over the ground.

I went up and turned the key off and said, "Go on up to the house with Mama. You're not big enough to drive the tractor by yourself, yet."

This hurt me a lot worse than it did him. It seemed real cruel at the moment, but it was a learning experience for both of us.

After about a week, Allen came to me and said, "Daddy, can you help me drive the tractor? I won't run over no more 'maters now, Daddy."

So the two of us got on the tractor and we worked with it till he mastered it 'cause now he was ready to take instructions. It wasn't long after that that he could drive that tractor just as good as anybody and he would find every excuse he could to drive it from giving his little dog a ride to cleaning up the yard. That Ford tractor was a fun thing for him.

It was also real hard to pay for 'cause those tomatoes were not as profitable as I had figured they would be. I think the best profit from owning that Ford tractor was in helping me to teach our boys about responsibility.

September was the month that the walnuts were ready to harvest. Me 'n Mama were always glad to see it come 'cause that was a time that we could get a little extra money to help get us out of the hole, or, at least ease the pressure a little bit.

We had about one hundred walnut trees in all. Some were big and some were little, with all sizes in between. As soon as the hulls on the nuts would start to shrivel a little, it was time to harvest them. The two older boys, Jim and Jerry, would climb up into the trees and hit the limbs with a rubber mallet so the walnuts would fall off the trees. Once in a while we would hire a walnut knocking machine to shake them off if we had the money.

The rest of us would pick them up in a bucket and take them over and put them on a table. Then all of us would take the hulls off of those that hadn't come off yet.

To say the least, this was not a job all of the kids liked. In fact, they all hated to do it. It was hard dirty, work. We all got our hands stained so black it would take several weeks for them to look right again.

Some times it was hot and some times it would rain. If it rained, we all had to get busy and get them up in a hurry 'cause if we didn't they would all split and spoil and we would get nothing out of them.

We would all line up under a tree and each one would take a path as wide as his or her arms could reach on both sides and we'd start down the row of trees. Even the little ones would have a little bucket to put their walnuts in. They would be praised for all the walnuts that they would pick up even if it might not be more that a half dozen or so. They were a part of the family, too, and they wanted to be included.

We all had rules to go by. When anybody had to go to the bathroom, we all went. When one of us got thirsty, we all stopped and got a drink. And when one of us didn't work like we were supposed to, we would get a walnut bounced on the head. When the buckets were full and were too heavy for the little ones to carry, the older boys would dump them.

Around noon, if everyone had worked real good, I would go down to the corner grocery store and buy a whole carton of ice cream bars. After lunch we would go back to work for the rest of the day while the little ones took their naps.

The neighbor just to the south of us had ten acres all in cherry trees. He had no children. He and his wife had to do all the work on his place. He would look over at our family all working together and would envy us because of our "free" labor. We know that was the way he felt 'cause he would mention it from time to time.

As the kids got older we felt that they should have a little cut out of the money that we got out of the walnuts, so me and Mama talked it over and we came up with this idea. We would take them on a trip on the Santa Fe Streamliner train to Oakland to visit with Grandy. The kids liked this idea and we spent some time talking about it and planning it. Everyone got in and worked real hard and we had a good harvest. It looked like we would have a lot of money and there would be some left over for our trip.

But it didn't happen that way. The price for the walnuts dropped way down and there was not even enough money to pay all of the bills we needed to pay. We sat down with the kids and explained the situation to them. They were all disappointed, but they went along with it. We told them that next year we would take them on the Streamliner trip after the walnut harvest.

But that was another bad year and me and Mama kept putting

off taking the kids on the Streamliner ride 'cause we just didn't have the money to do it.

They never did get that Streamliner trip. Now every time we all get together, someone brings up the subject and asks us when we're going to take them all to Oakland on the Streamliner train.

So it all goes to prove that there is a time to do things, and if you don't do them then, you may never get that chance again.

Walter with the kids hauling in tomatoes.

Chapter Forty-six

FEEDING THE KIDS

By now all of the little ones had come to live with us. In other words, we had a whole house full of kids, eight of them in all, four boys and four girls, and they were consuming a lot of groceries. It seemed to me that that was all that they did. No matter what I brought home, it was gone in nothing flat. All of the money that I could bring in seemed like it was not enough. I felt like the harder that I worked the more behinder we got. So I started a-lookin' around for a better way. I either had to make more money or spend less and I could not see how I could do either. So I started a-lookin' around to see if I could find some bargains that would help the money that we had go a little further.

It was in the winter time and I was plastering. It started to rain and I had to go home. Every day, on my way home, I passed by the wholesale milk and cheese place. It came to my mind to stop in there on this rainy day and see if I could get some long horn cheese at a little better price than we were a-payin' for it in the grocery stores.

There was no one in there except a man in the office and he came out to wait on me.

I said, "I came in here to see if I could get some cheese wholesale. I don't have an grocery store or anything like that, but I do have a whole house full of kids and I'm having a hard time of making enough money to feed them. Now don't get me wrong. It is not your fault that I have all of these little kids, but I thought maybe, just maybe, I could qualify for some price break on a few items that we use a lot of. Why, don't you know, when I bring home a five pound chunk of cheese it is gone in just a day or two."

Well, we talked there for a while, then he said, "How much do you want to get at a time?" And he told me the prices of things.

I took out my wallet and took a look at how much money that

I had and said, "Well, I can get this much."

He said, "That is just right. That will buy you a box of four long horns of cheese. That's a little cheaper than I get for it at the grocery store. Now, that price is just to you and don't tell all of your neighbors. If you do, I can't sell it to you any more. If you'll drop in from time to time, I might have some real bargains for you. I admire a man that has a big family. Me and my wife could never have any kids."

I went away from there feeling rich. Now I had enough cheese to last them a while.

In a couple of days I dropped in there again and he was glad to see me.

He said, "I have a lot of ice cream. We took over a new store and we gave them credit for the ice cream that they had on hand of another brand. Can you handle it?"

I said, "How much do you have."

He answered, "Oh, there is quite a lot of it. I guess there is a couple hundred pounds or so and I will let you have it all for five dollars."

It was too good of a bargain to turn down, so I said, "I will take it!"

I went across the street to the freezer locker plant at Orvis and Clingers and rented a locker and put all of the ice cream in it. That box was filled up! Now we had enough ice cream to last a little while, of every flavor that you could imagine.

The next time I went into the cheese place, the man asked me for my telephone number so if and when he had something, he could call me. This time he had some out-dated cottage cheese that he just gave me. I couldn't see anything wrong with it so I took it home. Even if there had been something wrong with it I could have fed it to the hogs.

One day, when I came home from work, he had called and said that he had a lot of those canned biscuits that were out-dated. So I stopped by and got them and we ate on them for a long time.

We also got out dated sour cream from him and Mama made a lot of good cheese cake with it.

One day when I stopped in there, there was a different man in the office. I figured that my source of good bargains was gone out the window. When I asked him what happened to the other fellow, he said that he was real bad sick. He had cancer and was not expected to live very long and that he was in a Veteran's hospital in the southern part of the state. But before he left, he told the new man about me and he said that I could carry on like I had been in the past. In fact, he even gave me better bargains than I was getting before. We got to be real good friends.

One day he said that he wanted to talk to me and for me to come into the office. This is how it went.

He said, "Walt, I have plenty of money, but life is not the same without any little kids running around the house. We have tried for years to have a family. Me and the wife have been talking it over and we figured that since you have so many kids and are having such a hard time of feeding them that maybe you would give us the two of the little ones. That way it would be a lot easier on you and your wife. I could give them a good education and that way they could have a real good life."

I interrupted him and said, "You gotta be kidding! That is the last thing that I would ever do." I got up and walked out. And this ended our friendship and my source of goodies at the milk and cheese wholesalers.

It was about this time that our good neighbor, Mr. Lyle, invited me to go to the farmer's market with him. He was taking some eggplant that he had grown down there. There was not a whole lot of it that he had to sell, but I think that he liked to go there to visit with a lot of the farmers and neighbors who lived around there.

I thought that it would be a lot of fun, so I said, "When do you want to leave?"

He answered, "Oh, about 11:30 tonight."

I thought this was kind of a funny time to go to the market, but I said, "Okay, I'll be ready."

He picked me up right on the dot and we took off for the farmer's market.

It was on Wilson Way, in the east part of Stockton. The market opened up at twelve midnight and all of the produce buyers for the grocery stores would come there to pick out what vegetables they wanted. I couldn't figure out why this was done in the middle of the night. Why couldn't his same thing be done in the day time?

Then my neighbor explained to me that the farmers had to work during the day and the store owners had to do the same thing.

189

When we got there, it was a big surprise to me. There were twenty-five or so farmers with their produce in the back of their trucks or pickups, backed up to form an isle. You could walk down and see what there was for sale on either side.

I never saw so much variety of vegetables and fruit for sale. Then, as it got toward morning, it got to be quite noisy around there. Every body was wanting to sell what they had left. Besides, if they took it home, all it was good for was to feed to the hogs. The best quality produce was sold first thing, and by the time it got daylight, everybody was getting ready to go home.

There was still a lot of good stuff left that I would like to buy, but I was riding with my neighbor and I didn't want to bother him by taking something home with me when he had come down there to sell his stuff.

I asked, "How often is this market open?"

He said, "Every Wednesday and Saturday."

I decided then that I would go to the Farmer's Market the next Saturday. With ten mouths to feed we could cut a lot of corners by buying here. It was a good place to get things real cheap at one time. On the next Saturday, I was back.

There was one farmer there who had a whole pickup full of strawberries that he hadn't sold. I was going to buy a crate of them for a treat for the family.

He must have been a-wantin' to sell them real bad, 'cause he said, "I'll sell the whole load to you for ten dollars."

Well, that was about all of the money that I had on me, but I couldn't pass by a bargain like that so I said, "Okay, it's a deal!"

When I pulled into the yard with all of those strawberries, Mama said, "Wow! That's enough strawberries to last us all winter." Then she kept all of the kids home from school to help her put them up.

After a while all the farmers there got to know me and knew that we had eight kids. From time to time we would get some real good bargains. I figured that it would be a good idea to make a walk-in refrigerator box to keep this stuff till we could use it.

So I built one in the back part of the garage. We weren't using it for a garage, anyway. My brother, Henry, was a refrigerator man and he came over and put the refrigerator part in it. It was a dandy. Now I bought whole boxes of apples, oranges, etc. I even bought a whole stem of bananas that had started to turn yellow. Now the kids could have any of this fruit that they wanted any time that they wanted to. There was only one rule about this, though. If they took it, they had to eat it all and not waste any of it. If they didn't, they weren't allowed to have any fruit for a whole week. They didn't waste very much!

This was one of the fun things that I liked to do – have a lot of good food to eat all of the time.

One night about one or two in the morning, someone knocked on our front door. There was a friend of mine with over one hundred pounds of green peas for us. He said that he and a friend had been a-workin' in a field close by harvesting peas. The harvester broke down and they couldn't work anymore that night. He had cleaned the peas out of the machinery. He knew his family couldn't handle them, so he brought them over to us. But they needed to be taken care of right away. They wouldn't wait till morning or they would heat up and turn yellow.

I thanked him for the peas and went back into the house and into the bedroom where Mama was trying to sleep.

She said, "Who was that?"

"Well," I said, "We have a lot of peas that need to be shelled and put into the freezer."

She said, "Okay. I guess we'd better wake the kids up to help us."

The kids grumbled, but they got up to help, and all of us shelled peas for the rest of the night. By morning we had enough peas to last us for a long, long time. That was one night the kids never forgot. Everyone got in and did his or her share to the best of his or her ability.

And this is how we went about getting enough groceries for all of those little ones.

In one corner of the kitchen we had a big barrel that held two hundred pounds of flour. We would make a trip to Modesto, about thirty miles away, just to buy the unbleached flour that we liked to use in making our bread. It would last about a month. We would go to the bakery and buy fresh yeast by the pound. It took about an inch cut off the block of yeast. I didn't measure the flour by the cupful. I measured it by the sifterfull. I didn't measure the liquid by the cupful. I measured it by the mason quart jarfull.

I used the milk bucket for making the sponge and letting it rise and a very large round dishpan that I used for mixing the sponge with the flour when making bread. I could bake only four loaves of bread at a time in my oven, so I divided the dough. I filled four bread pans and let them rise. When I put them into the oven, I filled another four bread pans to rise. When I took the first batch out of the oven, I put the third batch in the pans to rise. It was an all day job.

We had a very large oak table in the dining room. There was enough room to seat twelve people. With only ten people in the family we were very comfortable sitting around it. Daddy sat at the east end of the table and I sat around the corner to his left. The four boys sat on the side to Daddy's right. Charlotte sat on the opposite end from Daddy and the other girls sat to my left.

The evening meal was the time for all of us to be together. There were not many days that did not see all of us sitting around that table at one time.

That table was the center of most of our family activities. The top began to get all scarred up so Daddy covered it with some linoleum. I used this table for kneading the twelve loaves of bread that I made every other day. The linoleum made a more sanitary surface and was much smoother than the wood surface.

That was the place the girls learned how to knead bread. That was the place where school homework was done, peas were hulled for freezing, corn and green beans were prepared for freezing, meat was cut and wrapped for the freezer, and fabric was cut for the making of dresses for the girls and me and shirts for the boys and Daddy. Babies were often bathed and dressed there. Children sat there while shoes were tied. It was around this table that family discussions were held.

Birthday dinners and parties were "happenings" around this table. We often had guests for dinner, especially after we joined the Church of Jesus Christ of Latter-day Saints. Then we often had from two to six of the young full-time missionary Elders sitting there with us. These were happy times that bound us all together.

There were many times when the decisions made while sitting around that dining room table changed the direction of our lives. It played a large part in the maturing process of each and every member of our family.

Chapter Forty-seven

THE CALF SCRAMBLE

Almost every year me and the two boys would go to the San Joaquin County Fair. This was a big time for them. They were a lot of fun to be with. Although we didn't have a lot of money to spend at the fair we always had a lot of pure joy. The most exciting thing that we took in was the 4-H auction. That is where all of the 4-H kids would sell their animals that they had raised.

It was a "fat" auction. I mean, people would pay as much as five dollars a pound for some of those animals. This was the way that the local businessmen had of advertising their products, mostly those who had a lot of money and wanted to help out the 4-H kids.

There were boys and girls competing for the highest "per pound" prices. The grand champion steer could bring as much as fifteen hundred dollars.

This made Jim and Jerry's eyes bug out. But we were always too poor to afford a good steer to start out with. I guess that the leaders could see that other kids had this problem, too. So it wasn't too long afterwards that they started the calf scramble each year so that some 4-H member could get a free calf to raise.

Some of the business men with money to spare would buy some 500 pound steers fresh off the range. They would take them to the fair grounds and turn them loose in a corral for the kids to catch.

There would be only one member from each 4-H group who could participate in the calf scramble each year and you had to be lucky enough to get your name pulled out of the hat. There were usually five kids for every steer. This was county wide and there were a lot of kids wanting to participate.

One day Jim and Jerry came home from a 4-H meeting so excited they could hardly talk. One of them had been chosen to be in the calf scramble. I think it was Jim. Now was their big chance to get rich. Both of them were already counting how they were going to spend their $1000 on, 'cause if one of them had anything, they both shared equally with each other.

I said, "Wait a minute. You haven't even caught the calf yet, and the spending of the money is a long ways down the road. What you need to do is to practice wrestling a calf in the corral."

The next evening, I looked out the window and they were out on the front lawn really fighting with each other.

I went out and stopped them and asked, "What started all this?"

"Well, Daddy," one of them said, "This is the way it is. We were practicing wrestling and Jim thought that he could whip me and I was not going to let him and we both got mad at each other."

I told them to give each other a hug and make up and if they wanted to practice wrestling that was okay, but not to get mad a-doing it.

Well, the time went by fast and the next Saturday was when the big calf scramble event was to take place at the fair grounds. There were tickets sold for this event. I mean it was a BIG thing and if you wanted to watch your boys wrestle a calf, you bought a fifty-cent ticket. Of course, all of the money they got off this event went to helping the 4-H clubs.

Just before Jim went into the one acre pen where the calves were to be turned out, he said, "Daddy, What shall I do?"

I said, "Jim, you don't chase after the calves. That is what all of the other kids are going to do. You head for the far corner and wait there till the other kids chase the calves down to you. As soon as this happens, grab yourself a calf and put the halter on him."

Now, you see, each of the kids had the same kind of a halter. It was a one-quarter inch rope halter, and the rules were that when a kid had his halter on his calf, it belonged to him, even if he could not hang onto it.

I also said to Jim, "The first thing that you do is grab the steer by the ear and ram the first two fingers on your right hand up his nose as far as you can get them and bend your fingers so that they can't come out. Then put your halter on and you will have it made. Then hang on for dear life."

Soon the calves were turned loose in the middle of this big pen. There were five judges there to watch the whole thing, to make sure that everything went according to the rules.

The whistle blew and the calves were unloaded and they were off a-running. Here was this whole load of calves running scared, some twenty yards ahead of the running kids. Jim was a-headin' for the corner as was previously planned. I will have to admit it sure looked funny for one boy running the opposite direction from everybody else. He was able to get all the way to the corner before the steers did. And here they came, all of those steers with all of those kids in hot pursuit.

Jim grabbed the first one that got close to him and hung on. He was able to get the halter on it. Then, all of a sudden, here came another kid along and gave Jim a big shove and took his steer away from him.

Boy, I was upset when I saw what happened. But this did not miss the eye of one of the judges and Jim soon got his calf back. I say calf, but it was more like a half grown white-faced Hereford.

Well, we had to find some way to haul it home. We didn't even have a trailer hitch on the car that we were driving at the time.

As I was going out the gate, here came Mr. Miller, the county 4-H advisor, who happened to live next door to us on Alpine Road.

He said, "Have you a way of getting that steer home?"

I said, "No. That is, unless we go and rent a trailer and a hitch."

He said, "I'll take it home for you." And he did.

Everybody in the whole family was happy for Jim. He had his 4-H calf to raise.

The next thing was getting enough feed for it. We had something like nine or ten months to get it into choice condition.

Jim and Jerry put all of the money they had into that steer, and me and Mama did the same. The time went by real fast.

Now, this steer had to be trained to lead and to be gentle. He had to be washed and brushed so he would look pretty for the fair. Both Jim and Jerry spent many hours taking care of their 4-H calf so he would be all ready for the fair.

One Saturday, Mr. Miller came out to look at the steer to see if there was anything that he could do to help the boys. He looked the steer over real good. I could tell by the way he looked that he did not like what he was seeing.

He pulled a face and scratched his chin with his hand and said, "Well, Jim, This steer in not fat enough to make it."

It sure looked good and fat to me.

"I'm afraid that you can't show him in the fair, Jim. I am sorry. I know that you are disappointed, but that is the way that it is."

I felt bad for Jim, but I felt good for me and the rest of the family. Here was our winters supply of meat for the freezer. And I do believe that that was the best tasting meat I have ever eaten. It did not last too long, 'cause Mama would cook up a big platter of steaks you could not see over for supper, but there was never any left over.

But the two boys took it real good and Jim said, "Next year Jerry, you can catch one and this time we will be able to show it in the fair."

Well, this is what happened. Jerry's name was drawn for the calf scramble and he did catch one. That is to say, he caught one and we struggled to feed it, also. But it never made it to the fair, either. But all in all, it was a good experience. These are the things that make men out of boys.

Jim and Jerry with their scramble calf

Chapter Forty-eight

THE WRESTLING MATCHES

Where we lived on Alpine Road about half way between Stockton and Linden put us in the Linden High School District. Linden is some fourteen miles east of Stockton. It wasn't a very big school. I think about five hundred students went there, mostly kids from the farming community. Our two big boys rode the bus most of the time 'cause I went the other way to work.

After school Jim and Jerry participated in sports. First off in the fall, it was football. Then during the middle of the winter it was wrestling.

Now this was fine with me except when there were bees to be moved. You see, we had a few hundred colonies of bees and this was one of the ways that we had of making ends meet. We rented them out to the fruit farmers to pollinate their crops, and there were a lot of times when we just **had** to move the bees. It was very important to me that we got those bees moved, and the boys were always willing to help me with the moving.

When they had a big game somewhere, it was very important to them, too. But we struggled through it some how during the football season until it was over.

Then came wrestling. Both of them liked this more than they did football and they came home with stories of how good they were. But then, they'd been working at it all their lives.

At first I didn't pay too much attention to them. I was preoccupied with making ends meet. Sports never enthused me very much, but I told them as soon as they made the semifinals, I would take time out to go watch them.

Well, that day finally came and we had to go to a little town a hundred miles or so south of Stockton. There were schools from all over the northern half of the state meeting there. I never saw so many boys a-wrestlin' all at once before in my life. There were

197

wrestling mats scattered all over that gym floor.

Listed on a blackboard were all of the boys names and who they were to wrestle. Most of these boys came from schools a lot bigger than Linden was. I said to myself, what chance do they have of getting anywhere?

I wanted to see them win, of course, and I was getting real excited when they won their first bouts. You see, Jerry was wrestling in the heavy weight division and Jim was in the next weight just below that. Jim had spent a lot of time and hard work reducing down so that both of them could wrestle. Otherwise, they would have had to wrestle each other and only the best one would get to go to the semifinals. Anyway, they had it all figured out.

It was hard for me to watch them both. Some of the time both of them would have a bout going at the same time. Then I would watch one for a little while and then watch the other one.

There were some great big boys there a-wrestlin' and I was sure that my boys would get beaten pretty soon.

Well, after an exciting day and it was all over, both of them were winners and were qualified to go to the finals which would be held in Gilroy a month later.

Needless to say, the two boys slept most of the way home. That is, after they wound down a little from all the excitement. And I had been just as excited as they were.

Now this was a big feather in the cap for the Linden School. Their team beat out all of those other schools that had a lot more boys to pick from, but those boys didn't move bees and mix mud for their dad to plaster, either.

Well, the boys were a-markin' off the days on the calendar and practicing with each other every night after school till the big day came, and that fell on a Saturday. It was a long drive down to Gilroy, so we started out real early in the morning.

When we got there we found that this school was a lot bigger than the one before, and it had a much bigger gym and there were a lot more boys. Where they all came from, I don't know.

When they all got started, Jerry was a-wrestlin' at one end of the gym and Jim was at the other end. It sure was a lot harder to watch them both this time.

After a while, Jim lost, but Jerry was still in there a-hangin' on. When it came down to the final man he was to wrestle, the winner this time would be the champion. I got so excited that for a while I thought that I was going to pass out.

When the bell rang, they were at a draw and they had to go into overtime to see who was the best. Both of them were a-gettin' pretty tired. Then Jerry lost by one point. He had let his man get away from him.

Jerry said after the match was over that his man was so sweaty and slippery that he could not hang on to him. But he felt good about it and so did I. He had given it all he had.

The only regret that I had was that I had not gone to support them in all of the other games they had been involved in.

I am sure that Mama was just as proud of them as I was.

After all of the wrestling matches were over, me 'n Mama got a letter from the Coach. It was during their Senior year. This is what it says:

LINDEN UNION HIGH SCHOOL

P.O. Box 538

LINDEN, CALIFORNIA

March 3, 1959

Mr. & Mrs. Walter Swan
Rt.1 Box 808
Stockton, California

Dear Mr. & Mrs. Swan:

I want to take this opportunity to thank you for allowing Jim and Jerry to participate in wrestling during the last three years.

I appreciate the fact that they have been able to participate wholeheartedly in the program.

I know that it meant considerable time away from home on occasions when you probably had work you would have liked to have them do.

I'm sure that through participation in wrestling Jim and Jerry have developed, not only physically but have also learned the importance of responsibility and the fact that success in life requires hard work.

It has been a distinct pleasure having Jim and Jerry on the team and we will miss them next year.

I deeply appreciated the very nice trophy the team presented to me during the rally last Friday. It's extremely rewarding to know that one's efforts are appreciated.

> Very truly yours,
> (sig) John E. Phillips
> Wrestling Coach

Jerry and Jim's Senior Pictures

Chapter Forty-nine

SPIRITUAL STRENGTH

It was early in the spring of the year in 1956. At this time we had a whole house full of kids, eight in all. Jim and Jerry would soon be sixteen years old. Charlotte was thirteen and Carol Ann was twelve. Allen was nine, Johnny and Merri Lou were five, and Linda was four.

At this time I was a-workin' at the Stockton State Hospital. There were several men a-workin' there, doing various things. Some were shoe makers, carpenters, bakers, and so on. They all had the same thing to do as I did. That was to get this work done and at the same time help the patients to get better.

When it came noon time we all got together in one of the buildings to eat our lunch, that is, if we did not go to the cafeteria. I think most of the men were like me. The cafeteria got old real fast and home cooking was a lot better, even though it was nothing more than a sandwich. It seemed like there were at least half a dozen or so of us there every day.

There were several things a-goin' on during the lunch hour. If you wanted to play penny ante poker or Pinochle or checkers there was a game a-going on. Or you could tell smutty jokes or talk about religion and philosophize, whatever suited you. Well, I tried them all and the only one that gave me any satisfaction was the latter.

One day we were discussing religion. There was just the two of us a-talkin' together at this time. There was Waring Hart and myself. The subject came up about his church a-buildin' a new building. Waring invited me to come help. I told him that I just plain wasn't interested. We had stopped a-goin' to church.

But he continued. He said that they were building a stake-house and I thought he meant a "steakhouse" – a restaurant where they were going to serve fancy meals.

I said, "Not me. You can count me out. I have all that I can do a-feedin' all of my little kids."

Then he went on trying to tell me all about his church. But I was not much interested. Besides I had to get back to work.

I said, "You can tell me about it some other time."

He asked me if he could send some friends of his out to my house some time to tell me about it.

I said, "Sure," and then I forgot about it.

Several weeks passed by and I had forgotten all about our conversation, when one evening there came a knock at the door. There stood two men. They identified themselves and said they were from the Church of Jesus Christ of Latter-day Saints. They had come to tell us about their church. I invited them in and they introduced themselves as Reid Burt and Leonard Meyer.

Mama put the little kids to bed and the older girls went out to the kitchen to do the dishes. Me 'n Mama and the older boys sat around the table with Mr. Burt and Mr. Meyer and we gave them our full attention.

They had not been there fifteen minutes, when I began to find that a lot of my questions were being answered. There was a good feeling that came over me that I had never felt before in my whole life. They stayed about forty-five minutes and left with a word of prayer. They made an appointment to come back the next week.

The next day my wife did not get much housework done, 'cause she spent most of the day a-lookin' up scriptures in the Bible to prove them wrong.

When I came home that night she said to me, "I thought that they were wrong but I can't find a thing that they told us that was wrong at all. Walter, do you know, I think they are right, but they will never convert me. I am a died-in-the-wool Baptist. You go ahead and listen to them if you want to."

They came back several more times and I could see what they were a-drivin' at. They wanted me to join their church, but what they were a-tellin' me was so different than anything that I had ever heard before that it was taking me a while to understand all that they had said since I was not brought up a-goin' to church.

I could feel that it was true, but on the other hand, I had some doubts, so I told them not to push me in the least little bit or I would have to ask them not to come back any more.

All they said was, "We will present to you the facts and you can make your own decisions."

Well, several months went by. They'd come by from time to time to invite us to some church function or other. It was a hard time of the year for us. We were so poor that we did not have any clothes that we were could wear to church, at least, that was the way we felt about it.

Christmas 1956 came and all of the kids got new clothes. We decided that we would go to church the next Sunday. We took a family vote and decided that we would go to The Church of Jesus Christ of Latter-day Saints instead of the Baptist Church.

We all got dressed up and went to church in a little building on Harding way in Stockton. We took up a whole bench in the center section when we all sat down, and, to say the least, we were noticed by everybody that came in that day. They made us feel like that was the place we belonged on Sunday and everything that was said was for our benefit, or at least, it seemed so to me.

A couple of days later was New Year's Eve and we were invited to attend a big social. We didn't realize that it was for the adults and teenagers only and we took our little kids with us. But no one said anything and we were treated like we were somebody special.

The next day, I went to the phone and called our missionaries and told them that I was ready to get baptized. The two older boys, Jim and Jerry, and I were baptized the following Saturday evening. Mama wasn't ready yet, but I guess her "wool" got redyed 'cause she and the two older girls, Charlotte and Carol Ann, and our middle boy, Allen, were baptized about six weeks later. The three little kids, Johnny, Merri Lou, and Linda were still too young to be baptized then.

From then on there has been spirituality in our home that we had never felt before, and we have felt the strength of it. We are ever so grateful for the truth and light and knowledge we have gotten for having listened to those two missionaries.

Here was another decision which changed the direction of our lives. Opening the door and letting two strangers come into our home was the beginning of the biggest change of direction we had ever made together as a family. And it was definitely for the better. Someone asked me the other day why we had left another church for this one. The answer is simple. Here we found the answers to all of our questions about our relationship to our Heavenly Father and our fellowmen.

Now, after thirty-seven years, we look back and wonder what our lives would have been like, had we not joined the The Church of Jesus Christ of Latter-day Saints. It has been a very wonderful experience for us. We wouldn't have changed it for the world! We have been very happy serving our Heavenly Father in whatever capacities we could, and feel it a privilege to do so. This decision is making a difference in our entire family, which now numbers ninety-eight people, including ourselves. It was a positive action decision.

This is a "lay" church. There are no paid clergy, so we all do the work. It wasn't long before Daddy and I held teaching and leadership positions. Through the years these teaching and leadership positions have changed from time to time, giving us more opportunity for service and growth in the Church and in the Gospel. We had gained the spiritual strength we needed to make our lives complete.

Our children and grandchildren have followed with us in our service to God. We thank our Father in Heaven for the many blessings He has given to all of us.

Our Family shortly after joining the Church

Chapter Fifty

TAKING THE BOYS TO COLLEGE

There was a feel of fall in the air a-lettin' everybody know that summer was almost over, and this was a big time for Jim and Jerry. The two of them had been a-dreamin' of leaving home and going away to college for a long time. They both had a little scholarship, although it wasn't very big, but it was a scholarship just the same. They were accepted into the Brigham Young University in Provo, Utah.

There was quite some discussion on how was the best way to get them there and it was decided that it was a lot cheaper for us to drive up there than it was to go any other way. The only problem with that was that we didn't have a car that we would trust to make the trip.

As soon as it was known that the boys were going to BYU, we got an offer from a friend to use his station wagon, and we accepted the offer. This way me 'n Mama could have a little vacation, along with it. We had never had a vacation by ourselves. We would leave the big girls to take care of the younger kids.

The boys had planned ahead and had reserved a very small apartment in the basement of a Provo elderly widow, so we didn't have that to worry about. We knew exactly where we were going.

Well, we got all packed up and were off for BYU on time. There wasn't much room left in that car after it was all packed and we got into it, but it was a fun trip and we all enjoyed every minute of it.

When we got to Provo and found the place where the boys would be a-livin', and they unloaded the car. It was as much fun to watch the expression on the boys faces as anything else. We just had to take a picture of them. They were so excited they could hardly stand it.

We all got dressed up and took a tour of the Brigham Young

205

University campus. We were very proud to be leaving our boys in such a fine place as that. And we took some more pictures.

After that was all over they could hardly wait for us to leave so they could get on with their own lives. They had been a-dreamin' about this for a long, long time. Saying goodbye was hard for all of us, but it didn't take us long when the time came.

Then me 'n Mama headed for home. We hadn't gone but a little ways when we got to talking about the old homestead down in southern Arizona, and how long it had been since we had seen it. We decided to swing by there to have a little more of a vacation.

We called the girls and asked how things were at home, and they told us there was nothing they couldn't handle. So we told them what our plans were and they said that would be all right with them.

We had taken along a camp stove and some food so that whenever we got hungry we could eat. We folded down the back seat and we had put a mattress in there so we could have a place to sleep. We had lots of room now that the boys weren't with us.

We would find a pretty place to stop and cook us a meal and when it got dark we would find a good place to pull off the road and sleep in the back of the station wagon.

On the way to Bisbee, one afternoon we were a-comin' out of the mountains just outside of the little town of Globe, Arizona, when we heard a funny sound a-comin' from the rear of the car. Just about that time we lost the power. It was not a-workin' at all. I pulled off to the side of the road and took a deep breath.

I said, "Well, what will we do now? Here we are broke down with no money to pay for a major repair bill and we must be at least twenty miles from town."

We sat there a-talkin' for a while about just what would be the best thing to do. After some discussion we decided to see if I could get a ride into Globe and get a hold of the Bishop of the LDS Church to see if there was any way he could help us.

So I stood along side of the road with my thumb in the air. This bothered me 'cause I never liked to bum a ride, but I had no other choice.

Several cars went by and I was beginning to feel panicky. We weren't driving our own car. We had messed it up, and it had to be fixed. Oh there were a lot of things a-goin' through my mind.

Then, a pickup pulled to a stop and the driver asked me if I needed some help.

I said, "I sure do! I would like a ride to Globe to see if I can find a Mormon Bishop."

He said, "Well, I'm the Stake President. Can I be of any help?"

I told him that we had just taken our two boys to BYU and were on our way home in a borrowed car and the rear end went out on us.

He said, "I think that we can handle this."

So he towed us into town, and we went by his house to let Mama off there. Then we went to a garage that was run by a member of our church. That man had our car all fixed up in a couple of hours. I told him I'd have to wait till we got back home to send him some money.

He said, "That won't be necessary. I'm glad to help a fellow brother who has just taken his boys to BYU."

We were very grateful for his help.

Well, me 'n Mama went on down to Bisbee and took a look at the old homestead. It hadn't changed much since we'd seen it last. Then we went by and visited with my sister, Hazel in Palominas. And we headed for home.

On the way we stopped by Yosemite National Park, something we had been a-wantin' to do for years. We entered the park from the Nevada side so it was a long narrow winding road before we got to the main tourist area. We stopped and enjoyed the deer and other animals. The scenery so beautiful we had to stop and take pictures. We took our time and had a pleasant trip through the park.

From there it didn't take us long to get back home. When we got home we found that the girls had done a good of taking care of the younger kids and everything was fine.

This trip, nineteen years later, was the real honeymoon we didn't get to take when we were just married.

Jim and Jerry with Mrs. Jolly

Jim and Jerry in Provo, UT
September 5, 1959

Chapter Fifty-one

THE KID'S CHAPTER

We are putting The Kid's Chapter here because the next chapter is the last one in this book, and we want to write it for you.

We have invited our children to write some of their memories down to add to our book, "me 'n Mama", because they are the heart of our story. They are presented here from the oldest child first, down to the youngest one.

JERRY'S STORIES

A Lesson Learned:

We had a neighbor who's name was Mr. McNear. He was a very nice older gentleman and we were good friends. It was during World War II when 'most everyone had a "victory" garden. We had a garden, as well, at our home.

One summer afternoon, my brother, Jim, and I and a neighbor boy went over to Mr. McNear's garden. He had some very beautiful cantaloupes in his garden. So I picked one for my father to show him. Jim picked one and the neighbor boy picked two and took them home. I can still recall that they weren't even ripe.

When we got home Daddy was quite upset with us for picking the cantaloupe. We felt his very strong disapproval. I don't recall exactly whether he spanked us or not. However, he did make us go back over to Mr. McNear's house and apologize to him.

I can recall knocking on his door. By this time I was really, really sorry.

I said to Mr. McNear, "I'm sorry I took your cantaloupe." And we returned two cantaloupes that were of no value. But we did say we were sorry.

Daddy was a wise man and he tried to make it better, so he went to the store and bought a smoking pipe for Mr. McNear who smoked a pipe at that time. Daddy wanted to do something about

209

the incident and make it better.

I can still remember it and I learned from that early incident in my childhood that you must be responsible for your actions, tell the truth, and do not take things that don't belong to you. Then when something does go wrong, you need to say I'm sorry and do something to make it better.

Learning to milk the cow:

One morning Daddy came in and said, "Boys, I think it's time for you to learn to milk the cow."

I was about five years old at the time and I was a pretty big boy for five, but I didn't know if I could learn to milk a cow or not. But I trusted my father and I went about to try to learn to milk the cow.

The cow that we had at that time, we called Brownie. She was an old Jersey cow and she gave very good rich milk. But, she was a very, very tough cow to squeeze milk out of. In fact, in all my years of milking a cow, from the time I was five years old until I went into high school, she was the most difficult cow to milk of all the cows we ever had. But she was a good cow and she was very patient with me and with Jim as we began to learn how to milk her.

This cow was so good that we could go out in the pasture with the milk bucket, stop her in the field some place, give her a little bit to eat, and she would just stand there in the field while we milked her. And I do mean we. Ordinarily a cow is milked from the right side. But, as you know, there are two sides to a cow. So I milked on the right side and Jim would get on the left side, trying to aim the squirt of milk into the bucket. On occasion, when we would milk her, we would miss the bucket and hit each other – sometimes on purpose.

Milking the cow became a daily responsibility each morning for one of us to do. We shouldered that responsibility with some reluctance. However, we became better at milking the cow and other cows as we grew older and took care of that responsibility. By milking the cow we developed some strong muscles in our wrists and hands and arms. So we were blessed with strength in our arms and hands for having done a task that was a normal every day task.

Mama's tender loving care:

I have a story about Mama now. In my early childhood

210

memories I always recall Mama being there for us when we needed her whether it was an earache, or to tuck us in bed, or to bandage a cut. She was always there for us with good teachings and good upbringing.

I recall one time when we went to the back of our property to climb an apricot tree. Jim had climbed up in the tree to get some apricots and I was on the ground. Jim found something in the tree which I learned later was called a clevis. It was a U shaped piece of iron about the size of a horseshoe. Jim threw the clevis down to me, but I missed it and it hit me right on top of the head.

It hurt like crazy and so I started for the house, which was about 200 to 250 yards away. By the time I got to the house the wound on the top my head was bleeding so much that I was covered with blood from head to toe. I ran into the house screaming. My mother gasped when she saw me because she didn't know what happened. But very calmly she stuck me under the water faucet in the wash tubs, washed off my head, and found that there was a little cut on the top of my head. She bandaged it and consoled me.

This story is about wrestling and boxing:

From that Jim and I were little boys we would wrestle on the floor and play with one another wrestling. Because we were about the same size, neither one of us could get a distinct advantage over the other one. Pretty soon we got so good at wrestling that we had to do it outside on the lawn.

Well, when we were growing up we didn't have a lawn at our house so whenever we had a chance to go to someone's house that had a lawn, we would wrestle around on their lawn and have a good time with it.

One day we were over at a friend's house, by the name of Ray Bridges and he had a nice lawn. I forgot how old we were at the time but I think we were about eight or nine. Jim and I were wrestling and we were being watched by the family. Jim beat me three times in a row and I got all upset about it and I didn't want to wrestle any more. And so we didn't wrestle for a long time after that.

Then, later on, when we got to high school we got to take wrestling in our Sophomore year in high school but the only kids big enough to wrestle with us in high school was each other. So both Jim and I were on the wrestling team in high school and we both did very well in wrestling. Because of the strength that we had gained from milking all those cows earlier on, we were strong in our hands and forearms and were able to muscle our opponents a good deal of the time.

I was never able to beat Jim and Jim was never able to beat me up to that point. An interesting note along the way is that I went on to become a champion heavy weight wrestler in high school. I got fourth in my Junior year and second in my Senior year at the State tournaments. Jim won the intramural championship at BYU the next year.

Now back to boxing a little bit:

When we were just little guys growing up, Mama didn't like to see us fight, but Daddy got us some boxing gloves. He didn't want to see us using our bare hands as we fought, so he would put the boxing gloves on us whenever we got a little too rough with each other.

He'd say, "All right now, BOX !" And we would box each other with those boxing gloves until we were both crying. Then he'd ask us if we were all done fighting. If we said yes he'd take off the boxing gloves and say, "Now hug each other and go play."

It didn't take too many times with that kind of situation before we didn't fight with each other very often.

I remember Mama around the corner in the kitchen when we'd be out in the living room boxing and really going at it, she'd be around the corner crying because we were boxing and crying, too. Mama was very sensitive.

I have one other special story about Mama and it was a very special time. We were living in the "middle" house on Alpine Road. I didn't know it at the time and Jim didn't know it either, but Mama was pregnant with Allen and she was very sick with morning sickness and pregnancy sickness and the whole thing.

But we knew that she'd been throwing up and was awful sick and was on the couch a good bit of the time. We wanted to fix something for her to eat. So we quietly went about it in the kitchen to fix her some hot milk and toast, her favorite breakfast. We brought it in to her while she was laying on the couch. She was so touched about it that she began to cry and she gave each one of us a great big hug and a kiss for it. She went ahead and ate the hot milk and toast. Then she felt better and she didn't throw up that day. And we were just so pleased with ourselves that we could help Mama feel better that day.

These are the kinds of stories and incidents that built up confidence and trust throughout our whole life of growing up in the Swan family. I hope that some of these contributions can be a help to the book because I'm so proud of my mother and father for what they are doing and what they have done with our family.

JIM'S STORIES

Maybe one of the reasons Jerry and I are so big today is the way Daddy treated us when we were growing up. Somehow we equated being big with being smart or important or some other positive trait. Anyway, whenever one of daddy's business acquaintances came to see us, Daddy would call us over and introduce us. Then he would ask his friend how old he thought Jerry and I were. The friend would always guess two or three years older than we really were. That made us feel proud. It was like giving us a shot of self-esteem. I guess daddy knew something then that psychologists are just finding out today – children grow better on praise than they do on criticism.

He did other things that made us feel important too. Whenever he could, he came to our wrestling matches. Lots of times he was the only parent there. But he came to cheer us on.

He always tried to be interested in what interested us. When Jerry and I were about nine, he took us to see the Stockton Ports play baseball. After we got into the stadium we found some seats right behind home plate, but they told us we couldn't sit there because those seats were reserved. Well, Daddy went right out to the ticket booth and traded our general admission tickets for reserved seats. I don't remember who won the game, but I remember the thrill of sitting right behind home plate. I remember seeing Harry Clements hit an in-the-park home run. Jerry and I thought we had Daddy hooked on baseball. The only thing he was hooked on was being with his boys.

He did other things that helped us build self-esteem, like

building us up in front of others. He would take us out on plaster jobs with him and put us to work. Then he would introduce us to the owner and brag on us for working so hard.

Every job was a learning experience and I am sure there were times Daddy would rather have left us home. I learned a lot about being careful the time I dropped a pair of tin ships on the top of a porcelain stove in the kitchen of a school we were plastering near Tracy. I learned a lot about making a mess in someone's driveway and patio the time I was cleaning up the wheel barrow outside a customers house in Stockton. I had white plaster water all over the sidewalk, patio, and driveway.

I learned about the seamier side of sex from one of Daddy's plasterers. The summer we were thirteen Daddy had a contract to plaster the Riviera Motel on Wilson Way in Stockton and he had hired Jerry and me to work as plasterers. At lunch one day we all sat down together and a man named Carl went into great detail about his experiences with a prostitute in Japan. I think he apologized to Daddy later. It didn't seem like a big deal to me, but after thirty-seven years I still remember what he said.

That was also the summer we learned about child labor laws. After the motel job, Daddy didn't have any more work so Jerry and I went to work for Ted. "Slim" was a good friend to Daddy and told Ted that he would work for him only if he would hire Swan's boys, too. Ted had a big job plastering some new building at the county fairgrounds. He put us to work scratch plastering I-beams covered with metal lath. We were on a rolling scaffold about eighteen feet above the ground. As long as we were working with Daddy, we were okay, but we had to be at least sixteen to plaster for someone else. Dave was casually visiting with a man who was responsible for enforcing child labor laws.

When Ted told him he had two thirteen-year-olds plastering for him, he said, "I didn't hear you say that, but if you do have two underage boys working, go get them and take them home." That was the end of our plastering career for a while.

Being in the limelight builds self-esteem, too. Jerry and I had our pictures in the paper before we were a week old. We were one of four sets of twins in the hospital at the same time we were born. Ten years later when Johnny and Merri Lou were born, we had our pictures in the paper again, twice. Once for being two sets of twins in the same family and the second time for being one of the events of the year. 4-H gave us opportunities to be in the limelight again. Jerry and I won a team demonstration contest two years running and we did a camp cooking demonstration on television.

Learning how to work and growing up believing that I could do anything I set my mind to, has made the difference in my life.

When we were growing up we had pigs, cows, chickens, bees, sweet corn and all kinds of garden projects – ostensibly to make money. Our 4-H project was a milk cow that Jerry and I learned to milk when we were five years old. We milked cows until we graduated from high school. I don't know if we ever made any money from the cows, but we sure developed some strong muscles – the kind of muscles you need to become a championship wrestler. I was never pinned in three years of wrestling in high school and I won an intramural wrestling tournament my freshman year at BYU.

Some of those muscles started the year Daddy bought cull potatoes for ten cents a hundred pounds to feed to the pigs. Jerry and I would come home from school every day and fill this big "cannibal" pot with potatoes and water and build a fire under it. Of course we had to empty the cooking pot and feed the potatoes we had cooked the day before to the pigs.

Once we drove some concrete reinforcing rods into the ground to support the cooking pot. The rigging worked fine until the fire got hot and weakened the rods. Then the whole mess spilled on the ground. Jerry and I sat down on the ground and bawled in frustration. We knew Daddy was going to be mad at us for not getting the potatoes cooked. But he wasn't! He came home and looked at the mess and said, "How can I help?"

One summer Daddy promised to take us fishing if we did our chores well, without being prodded. We had a one-bedroom rental house next to our house that nobody was living in at the time. So we asked if we could "sleep out" in the "little house". It was okay and we felt all grown up. We were so excited about doing our chores well that one morning we got up before daylight to start our chores. Daddy heard us outside and asked what we were doing. We said we just wanted to get an early start on our chores.

He said, "Go back to bed boys. It's only 3:30 in the morning."

That wasn't the last time we got up before daylight to do the chores, but from then on we knew what time it was.

The summer that we were ten, we sold sweet corn in front of the house for forty-five cents a dozen. We bought our own school clothes that year and every year thereafter. It was a sense of pride with us. Only a few of our friends ever bought their own school clothes. It seemed that Daddy always figured out a way for us to make money.

During the Korean War we raised a crop of tomatoes. Tomato prices were higher that year ($32 a ton) than they had ever been before. It took several years for them to reach that price again. We picked most of the tomatoes ourselves and hauled them to the cannery on a four-wheel trailer Daddy rigged up to pull behind our 1938 Plymouth. The trailer could only hold four of five boxes high and one pallet wide.

At the cannery they would weigh our load and randomly inspect our tomatoes. If the tomatoes were too green, moldy, sun scalded or rotten they were unsuitable for canning. The inspector would dock our load depending on the percentage of bad tomatoes in one box. The inspector could not inspect a box he could see and he couldn't take one off the bottom row. The last load we took to the cannery was only one row of boxes high. Since he couldn't select a box for inspection he could see, the inspector asked Daddy to pick two or three boxes for inspection. Daddy picked some boxes he knew Jerry and I had picked. The inspector found one or two blemished tomatoes in each box. Daddy said to him, "You know, my boys have been trying all year to get a perfect load." The inspector said, "Aw. What the heck!" and didn't dock the load at all.

When we were eleven we got started in the bees. Daddy would go all over the county collecting swarms for people. They were glad to get rid of the bees. He could have charged them, but he didn't.

One time we went to get a swarm near Linden. The bees were well settled in a hollow, square pillar on the front porch. We had to take off two sides of the pillar to get to the bees. Daddy took the honey comb out in sections, cutting it to fit into regular hive frames. Then with two or three wraps of a string he held the comb in place. We ended up with six or seven frames of brood and honey. The bees would repair the comb and attach it to the frames. It took about two hours plus travel time to collect that swarm.

Early in our bee career, Daddy read an ad in the Stockton Record for some bees for sale. The next Saturday we traveled to Valley Home to meet Miles Ponton and Johnny Clemons. They had 400 hives they wanted to sell. We didn't have the money to buy the bees, but Daddy went to work for them taking off their honey and extracting it. It was on one of these honey robbing expeditions that I became inoculated to bee stings.

Bee stings leave a small amount of venom in the victim. Swelling usually occurs. Well, we had gone to a clover seed farm near Valley Home to take off some honey. It was a cool and windy day in the early fall. The bees were loaded with honey, but they were all in the hive ready to defend their stores. It was too windy outside to be gathering honey.

Standard procedure for robbing bees in those days was to shake as many bees from a frame of honey that was ready to harvest and brush the rest of the bees off with a stiff brush, then replace the full frame with an empty one of honey comb. The idea was to trade the bees empty frames for full ones. We would make a stack of supers on the ground near the hives, then load them on the truck. It was important to keep everything "bee tight", otherwise the bees would "counterattack" – robbing their own honey back. This isn't a big deal on a hot day with a good honey flow. The bees are working the blossoms and are only mildly concerned about intruders stealing their honey. But on a cold windy day, watch out! Especially if you aren't wearing gloves.

Though we had done it a few times before, Jerry and I were both inexperienced at robbing bees. A robbery got started on the truck. The only way to solve the problem is to get in the truck and drive off. We couldn't do that because we had to finish the job. Somehow we got through, but when we got home that night my fingers were so swollen from bee stings that I could barely move three of my ten fingers. The rest were swollen stiff to about twice their normal size. From then on, I never swelled up from a bee sting. They still hurt, but I had bee venom immunity for life.

I still remember times we took honey off the bees all day and then stayed up most of the night extracting it while it was still warm. The bees taught us a lot about perseverance and staying with a task regardless how painful it was or how tired we were.

It wasn't all pain. Whenever we went out to work the bees, we always had to put gas in the truck. Daddy stopped at Joe's for gas and always came out with a treat, usually a bag of candy or whatever caught his eye. On the way home we usually stopped for a soda or an ice cream bar.

Jerry and I had this brotherly rivalry about riding by the window. It wasn't like you think. Whoever sat on the outside was the "okie." He had to get out and open the wire gate – which we commonly referred to as "okie" gates. In order to do their job of keeping the cows in, the gates had to be tight. Opening and closing a tight wire gate is difficult if not painful. You have to use your shoulder and pull against the fence post to tighten the wire and loosen the wire loop that holds the gate in place. Jerry and I had lots of fun jockeying for position to avoid being the "okie." But the "okie" never had to be "smushed" in the middle and he got more of the benefit of having the window rolled down in the summer.

I don't think we ever made much money from the bees, but sometimes the "honey money" was the only money in the house. It got spent for whatever the family needed. Now that I think about it, Daddy didn't have all these supplemental projects to make money. While they did provide food for the family, they never did produce the cash we all dreamed about. Daddy cared more about raising children who knew how to work than he did about making money. When I think of the quality time he spent with us – hours in the truck riding all over the country to tend to this job or that one, the quiet spring days working bees – I know now he knew what he was doing, even if Jerry and I didn't. He was giving his sons everything he had to give – himself.

The year we were twelve, Jerry and I got a basket ball for Christmas. It seemed like we always had scrap lumber around the place, so we rigged a basketball goal on an old redwood telegraph pole. We didn't care if the boards fit tightly as long as they touched. Neither did we mind if there was no concrete pad to play on. I was still on crutches from my leg operation. Daddy got out there with Jerry and me. We didn't believe in his shooting ability, but he held his own and we all had a good time together.

Mama always stayed home. She listened to us. None of us had the courage to talk back to Daddy when we thought we had been mistreated. So we told Mama how we felt. She never took our side, she just listened and somehow things would get better.

218

I don't ever remember Mama and Daddy fighting in front of us kids. But I do remember a few misunderstandings which lead to hurt feelings. One such misunderstanding was over cooking chickens.

It seems as though we always had chickens on the farm for eggs and meat. It was not uncommon for daddy to slaughter and dress a chicken or two for the evening meal. One time he brought a nice, but old hen into the kitchen for supper. Mama cut it up and fried it. Boy was it tough! Daddy got upset and told Mama she should have made chicken and dumplings with the hen.

A few weeks later he brought two pullets (fryers) into the kitchen for supper. This time Mama made dumplings with them. By the time Daddy got through explaining how to tell the difference between a fryer and a stewing hen by the amount of cartilage on the breast bone, Mama was to the point of tears. Daddy went out on the back porch and sulked because he had hurt Mama's feelings.

On Memorial Day, 1950, Daddy white-washed a house in Linden. It was so hot that he suffered a heat stroke. He was unable to work for a long time and gradually went into a period of depression. His illness affected the whole family. But there was very little we could do to make things better for him. One morning one of the kids came running into the house and shouted, "Daddy is whistling!" It had been a long time since we had heard that. But to everyone in the family it was a signal that Daddy was getting better.

Latter Daddy admitted the turning point for him was realizing that he had to help himself if he was going to get well. He decided to act **as if** he were feeling better and maybe that would really make him better. He started by whistling. This lead to other cheerful behaviors and he finally cured himself of his depression.

Mama nursed us when we were sick. We all had all the childhood diseases they have shots for now (German measles, red measles, mumps, whooping cough, etc.) Plus, we had several bouts with tonsillitis. About the only side benefit of being sick was staying in bed all day and getting to listen to the radio. I remember having the mumps. It was particularly difficult to swallow. I remember eating some frozen smoked shad. It tasted great, but it was painful to swallow. Mama let us go back to school the day before Valentines Day. Boy! Did we take a ribbing at school!

We were always trying to surprise Mama. Mother's Day and her birthday on June 30th were our favorite targets. Rarely did we buy her anything personal, though I do remember buying her a pink gingham shirtwaist dress at Mode-O-Day once. She usually got something for the kitchen. One year when I was in my poetry phase (about 15 or 16), we gave her an ice cream freezer filled with ice cream ready to eat for her birthday. Daddy had schemed with us to get her out of the house while we prepared the surprise dinner. On this occasion he was going to take her out to dinner and the movies. They got all the way into town when Daddy discovered he had left his wallet at home. (Not an uncommon occurrence, but this time it was on purpose.) The trip to town took about thirty minutes. So we had an hour to prepare a meal and make the ice cream. Everybody pitched in and did their part. Jerry, Allen and John made the ice cream. I fried the chicken and made the gravy and the girls made the mashed potatoes and the rest of the meal. We were ready when mama and Daddy returned.

What a surprise! I don't know if Mama thought very much of the ice cream freezer, but I know she loved our thoughtfulness. She especially liked the poem I wrote to go with the gift. She laughed and cried as she read all ten verses. I remember making a lot of homemade ice cream that summer.

(Here is Jim's poem, with his spelling.)
HAPPY BIRTHDAY MAMMA

This gift of ours
We give with pleasure
With lots of fun
That will not measure.

We surched and surched
It seemed forever
Until we found this gift
That will last forever.

Not in body
But in sperit
This gift of our
Has one fine merit.

To do its job
And remembered well
With all those thing
That looked so swell.

The gift itself
Cannot be thanked
There has to be someone
To turn the crank

By now we hope
You have guessed our suprise
The ice cream it makes
Can be served with pies.

This gift we give
To you our MOTHER
That we wouldn't swap
For any other.

Christmases were usually sparse in our home. Plastering work was slow in the winter, so about all we could do was pool our money and draw names to buy each other $5.00 gifts. Sometimes we would hold back a sack or two of nuts from the walnut harvest in the fall. We sold the nuts for Christmas money.

The Christmas of 1955 was one such Christmas. I was fourteen and into writing poetry. All I wanted was a rhyming dictionary. Mama made sure I got one. I wasn't surprised, but I was sure happy with my Christmas gift. It was one of the most meaningful gifts I ever received. Since then, when selecting a gift for someone, I have tried to match my gift to the interest of the person.

With as much care and concern as Mama and Daddy had for us kids, it wasn't a surprise that they embraced the gospel as taught by The Church of Jesus Christ of Latter-day Saints. Jerry and I were fifteen and on the verge of making some important life choices. Getting drunk was my goal for my sixteenth birthday. Of course it never happened because we had joined the Church. Instead we went to the A&W and had a hamburger and a root beer

221

float. We had become involved with the youth at church and their wholesome activities. They took us right in and made us part of the dance festivals and road shows. They put us to work and taught us the gospel.

The Church transformed our lives. So much so that our relatives and friends noticed it. Grandy, (Daddy's mother) noticed it so much that she joined the Church soon after we did. So did Uncle Henry and his family.

When Jerry and I graduated from high school, Daddy got us jobs with plastering contractors and we earned enough money for our first year at Brigham Young University. After the first year, Daddy got sick and Jerry and I had to come home and get jobs to support the family for a few months. About seven or eight months later I went back to BYU and Jerry got married a month or two after that.

CHARLOTTE'S STORIES

My earliest recollection was of a time when Mama asked me to gather the eggs from the hen house. It seemed like such a long way from the house. It was a wooden building about six feet by six feet. There were lots of nests in wooden boxes. It was fun to gather the eggs because there were different colored eggs – brown, green, and white. It was like an Easter egg hunt.

I must have been about four years old because I was allowed to run around in my underpants during the hot summer months. When I got there, I discovered that I hadn't brought anything with me to put the eggs in. I had seen my mother gather up the corners of her apron to collect the eggs. So I decided that since I didn't have an apron on, I could just put them in my panties.

Mama was quite surprised when I brought the eggs to her. I tried not to break any of them by walking carefully, but some of them broke anyway. Mama laughed and hugged me and told me that maybe next time I should take something to put the eggs in.

When I was eight I remember Mama being pregnant with twins. To me she seemed huge. I figured she must not feel well or maybe she was just tired because she laid down on the couch a lot. My young mind did not understand completely her condition, but being the oldest girl in the family, I knew I had to help her.

Mama usually made bread about every other day. When she was too tired to do it herself she began to teach me. She would instruct me every step of the way as she lay on the couch.

Kneading the dough was an enormous task for my small hands. I would get tired of kneading the dough before it was smooth. I remember gathering the entire mass of dough in my arms and carrying it to Mama to ask her if I had kneaded it enough.

I was always glad if Daddy came home when I was kneading the dough because he would finish the job for me. His hands were so large and strong, it seemed to me that he could finish the job in an instant. The best part of making the bread was getting to punch down the dough. We baked twelve loaves every time we made bread.

Later, after the twins were born, I remember coming home from school and Mama would have hot bread just coming out of the oven. Mama always let us tear off the top of a hot loaf. There was always plenty of fresh homemade butter and jam to put on it. This was my favorite treat when I got home from school. I was glad she let us kids eat this way. She never fussed at us at all about destroying a loaf of bread.

When I was about twelve years old, I wanted a horse more than anything else in the world. When Daddy brought home a beautiful horse one day, I was ecstatic. I didn't realize it at the time, but Daddy made a lot of sacrifices just to get his little girl a horse. At first I rode my horse everywhere, but then, as with most kids, I lost interest and I rode the horse less and less. Daddy warned me that if I didn't ride her more and take better care of her that he was going to sell her. Then one day, the horse was gone. I wish, now, that I had been more appreciative of my Daddy's love for me.

During the summer months, it seemed to me that we girls and Mama were always canning or freezing something – corn, string beans, berries, peaches - lots of peaches, apricots, jam, pickles – whatever Daddy grew in the garden or got a good deal on from one of the farmers.

We were canning apricots one day and it seemed to me that we would never finish. Mama must have felt the same way because toward the end of the day she surprised me by yelling out in an excited voice, "I found it! I found it!" I asked her what she found and she said, "The last apricot!"

I am forever grateful to my parents for teaching me the value of working hard, loving my family and neighbors, helping those in need, sharing with others and keeping God's commandments.

Thank you Mama and Daddy for giving me life and being great parents. I love you.

CAROL ANN'S STORIES

It was February of 1953. Mama was about to have a baby and my birthday was coming very soon. I would be eight years old. There was no money for buying me a gift. That was a little hard for me to understand and accept, but I thought if that baby were born on my birthday, it would be a great birthday present.

I'm sure I reminded Mama ten times a day that I wanted that baby to come on my birthday. She said she would be happy if that happened, but she couldn't make any promises. Babies came when they were ready.

My birthday came on February eighth, a bright, but very windy Sunday. Daddy ask me to go with him to run some errands. He wanted to find some berry plants he could put in the garden out in the back. We went several different places. I didn't mind. It was my day to be with Daddy.

By noon we were back home and I ran into the house to find Mama. I was sure she would be wanting to go to the hospital to have the baby.

I found her, but she said it wasn't time yet. About every half hour I would ask her if it was coming yet. By late afternoon I realized that she was not going to have that baby on my birthday. I was disappointed.

Mom and Dad Robinson came out to see us and give me my only birthday gift, a flannel night gown that my grandmother had made for me. I went to bed early that night so I could wear the new night gown.

The next day about noon, Mama suddenly announced that she was ready to go to the hospital to have the baby. Daddy was at work, so Aunt Ruby came and took her to the hospital. Mama called Daddy and I guess he got there in time.

Anyway we were delighted when we found out we had a little

sister. Mama and Daddy chose the name of Linda Lee for her. We were really happy about that because Charlotte and I had strongly suggested that name.

A neighbor and friend, Ermaline Tribuna, came over to take care of us while Mama was in the hospital. I don't remember too much about her except that she made good soup. She was with us when Daddy left to bring Mama home from the hospital.

He must have been very anxious to get her home because he left without taking the bag with the clothes she was to wear home.

Ermaline took the clothes and ran to her car and chased after him. She finally caught up to him about four miles from home. We all laughed for a long time about that.

Linda arrived home safely and we were so glad to have her and Mama home. A few days later, when Linda was only thirteen days old, Mama noticed the baby wasn't breathing right.

When she told Daddy, he said, "Let's go to the hospital."

It was a long distance away. By the time they got there, Linda's lips and fingernails were turning blue from lack of oxygen.

The rest of us children were waiting at home for their return. When they did come through the front door, Mama had Linda's baby blanket wrapped up around her arms like there should have a baby there. My heart sank when I saw she didn't have the baby with her. I thought she had died. They told us she would have to be in the hospital for a while.

Every year on Washington's birthday, Mama and Daddy would measure and mark our heights on an upstairs closet door. We did this while Linda was still in the hospital that year.

I remember one parent saying, "Shall we mark the door for Linda using her birth length?"

The other said, "Maybe we should wait to see if she lives or not."

The first one said, "She is still our baby and her name belongs here."

We were all very relieved when Linda was able to come home again and be a part of our family.

Mama worked so hard to take good care of all of us. Some how the day would be gone before she could get everything done. There were times when the clean washed sheets were not back on the bed when it was time to go to bed. I'm sure Mama was tired.

She would tell us she would make up the bed around us. She would put the bottom sheet on the bed and let us lie down. She told us to lie very still and she would make the bed up over us.

I loved this special time. I knew my mother loved me. To this day, when I smell a nice clean sheet, fresh from the clothes line, I think of her love for me. There are many ways to say I love you.

As a small child, I would get deathly car sick when we went very far. It wasn't something I could do anything about, but it usually gave me a place in the front seat of the car. That is a very desirable place when there are eight children. We didn't always have a car. Sometimes we only had a truck.

About once a year, we would go for a picnic. It would take all morning to get ready and then we would go to the foothills east of Linden. We would go to San Andreas, Mokelumne Hill, Jenny Lind, or the like. Then, again, I got to ride in the front. Curves were very rough on motion sickness.

We would have a great lunch of fried chicken and potato salad. We could always invent games to play.

On one such occasion, I was about seven and Jim and Jerry and Charlotte were having great fun hiking up a hill a hundred yards or so and running down. I wanted to play, too. I hiked up and started to run down, but I soon had a big problem. I was going faster than my legs were and I was soon tumbling head over heels.

I managed to stop, but I was very upset.

I heard Daddy call from the bottom of the hill, "Get up and try it over again."

I wasn't about to. Yet, when I tried to walked a short distance, I found myself tumbling again. I was so upset I cried.

Daddy came and rescued me and hugged me better and gave me a big piece of a giant Hershey bar for my efforts.

ALLEN'S STORIES

I was fifteen years and ten months old. I had a California driving learner's permit, which I had had since I was fifteen and a half. However I had been driving tractors and trucks since before I can remember.

I can recollect having to jump off the tractor seat onto the clutch and bounce up and down with all my weight to change gears.

I was driving before I ever learned to ride a bicycle!

When I was in the sixth grade, I was earning money by disking under weeds at the grade school and in neighbor's yards. I drove a lot of off-road miles helping my father move bees in the cherry orchards.

About that same time I got a job with a local septic tank installer who had a fleet of about thirty-five or forty World War II trucks and pieces of equipment. It was my responsibility to be sure they all had gas and oil, check the tires, and put water in the batteries. Of course, this necessitated driving them around in the yard. For this I was paid fifty cents per hour. This wage was minimal in comparison to the enjoyment I got from being able to drive.

When I was fifteen my parents decided to move to Pima, Arizona. My father had a 1962 Chevy flat-bed one-ton truck, and I had a burnt orange 1952 International pickup which was the joy of my life. My dad rented two National Rental closed-in trailers and we loaded them with as many of the necessities a large family requires as they could hold and started off for Arizona. My mother agreed to ride with me in the International so I could drive.

The highways, then, were narrow two lane roads that passed through occasional small towns in the desert and larger "freeways" in the big cities of Bakersfield, Phoenix, Tempe and Mesa where the top speed was fifty miles per hour.

It was the middle of September. School had already started, but it was still well into 100 degree weather. We made stop after stop for gas and water and to eat peanutbutter and dill pickle sandwiches on homemade bread. There was no money for restaurants or motels. That trip seemed endless – at least "a month long" to me. Probably five days in actuality.

I vividly remember driving through Apache Junction, Arizona on the way up to Globe. There are still gas stations here today that I remember seeing thirty years ago. I especially remember a Chevron station at Ironwood and Apache Trail that has just recently closed.

The Superstition Mountains faced me as I traveled down that road. How impressive they were, so rugged and colorful in comparison to the mountains I had left behind. I couldn't believe that anyone could live in such a dry arid place.

Today I live just outside Apache Junction. I have worked at the foot of the Superstition Mountains many days since 1981, and it is still just as impressive. I can't imagine living any where else, now.

I drove every inch of that road from Stockton to Pima in that International truck – several times, as it took many trips to move all of our belongings.

Today I own a 1952 International pickup just like the one I drove as a teenager. This one is metallic blue-green. It doesn't run. The weather and time have eaten away at its upholstery and its rubber tires. It is rusty in spots, but it is my dream to one day restore and drive that truck over the same road that I traveled from Stockton to Pima so many years ago.

JOHN'S STORIES

Looking back from the plus side of forty at my childhood years, many adventures come to mind. However, the two things which stay with me the strongest is that my parents were always there for their children and no matter what happened they provided love, shelter, and food for us.

Mom would spend most of her day in the kitchen preparing meals and baking, while Dad, if he wasn't at work, would be out in the garden or tending the livestock.

Due to economic needs, our days would often start early. The boys would be out in the barn milking the cows and tending the livestock while the girls would be in the house helping Mom with breakfast. After school there were always more chores that needed to be done, and they were often the responsibility of the entire family.

The garden was a family project and was always needing to be planted, weeded, watered, or harvested. We also had fruit and nut trees that needed pruning or picking.

As a child living on that small farm in California, participating in the welfare of our family, I have learned the value of hard work as well as the resulting knowledge that there is always a reward for my labors.

At forty plus years, I have learned that love, hard work and perseverance have empowered me through the journey of life. The quality of my living has been, in part, due to my family and the love and sorrow we all shared and bore together. Thank you Mom and Dad.

MERRI LOU'S STORIES

December was an exciting time for me as a child. My birthday is in December and two weeks after that is Christmas. Although Christmas was usually quite slim around our home it was still fun and exciting.

One of the neatest things about Christmas was when Daddy would drive around the nicer neighborhoods so we could see all of the beautiful Christmas lights. We would sit in the back seat of the car peering out the window "ohing" and "ahing" at every house with Christmas lights. We usually took this drive on a Sunday night on our way home from church. By the time we arrived back home we would be cold and hungry, so Mama would make us hot chocolate and cinnamon toast.

One particular Christmas we were quite poor. It looked like we were not going to even be able to have a Christmas tree. Then someone came up with the idea of going up into the hills and getting a mansanita tree. So that is exactly what we did. It was the prettiest little non-green Christmas tree I ever saw. We must have had lots of Christmas trees, but that is the one I can remember the most.

This same Christmas, Mama told us not to put our stockings up because Santa Claus was not going to be able to fill them this year. I was at the age when I figured that there was no real Santa, but I still wanted to believe. So I decided to put it to the test. After everyone went to bed, I quietly tip-toed into the living room. I draped my stocking over the woven basket that stood beside the fireplace. The next morning I couldn't wait to check my stocking. Yet, I was also a little apprehensive about finding out the truth. Making sure no one was watching me, I made my way to the stocking. I reached for it only to discover it's emptiness. I was disappointed but not surprised. I had received my answer, NO SANTA CLAUS!

When I just a little girl, probably about six or seven years old, my grandma, whom we affectionately called "Grandy", lived next door to us. Our houses were about a hundred feet apart, with no sidewalks in between because we lived out in the country.

Grandy had a television set. On occasions she would ask us kids to come and watch TV with her. This was a real treat for us because we didn't have a TV. She usually watched shows like *Gun Smoke, Raw Hide*, and *Wagon Train*.

One chilly rainy fall night, we were invited over to watch TV. The sun had gone down and night had set in. Johnny, Linda, and I started out the front door. We decided to run because of the cold, the rain, and the dark. We ran along the side of the road, with me trailing behind, for some reason. That one hundred feet seemed like a long ways to a little kid in the dark so I decided to sprint the last few feet.

As I approached the house I started down a slight slope from the road. The grass was wet from the rain and I slipped and fell. The fall wasn't so bad, but it was the mail box that I hit with my chin that hurt. I stood up and discovered I was bleeding. I turned around and ran back home.

I was crying pretty good by the time I reached the front door. Daddy took one look at me and said, "That chin needs stitches!" I had never had stitches before. I wasn't sure what was in store for me. All I knew was that I was scared to death.

"Daddy, I don't want any stitches. I'll be okay." I said whimpering.

My father, in his great wisdom, said, "Lou Lou (that was what he often called me) if we don't get that sewed up you will end up with a bad scar for the rest of your life."

Well, it appeared that I had no choice in the matter and if that was the case I wanted someone else to go with Daddy and me. Since I was hurt, I wanted a lap to lay my head on on the way to the doctors. But to my disappointment, everyone else was busy doing other things. Mama had to stay with Johnny and Linda. Charlotte, my biggest sister, was gone on a date. Carol Ann, my next biggest sister, was getting ready to leave for a date, too, and the big boys were gone. But that was okay since their laps weren't very gentle. What was I to do? There were no laps available to lay my wounded head on.

Carol Ann, being the sensitive sister that she is, called her boyfriend and told him that her little sister needed her and asked him if he could come for her about an hour later than they planned.

I was so glad and I felt comforted that she was going with me. I shall always remember the act of kindness she gave me that night.

Our first summer living in Bisbee, Arizona on the Swan Ranch, I became acquainted with southern Arizona thunder storms. According to Mama and Daddy it would be great fun to sit in the car and watch the storm roll in and give it's grand performance. As for me, I wasn't too sure about the idea. I have always been afraid of lightening storms.

Daddy coaxed us into watching from inside the car. I must admit it was a magnificant sight as the big billowy clouds came crashing together, but the loud crackling of the thunder and the lightning that darted across the sky frightened me to death. I wanted no part of this, nor did I want to stay in our underground house all alone.

John and Linda said they would come with me. (They were probably just as scared as I was.) We ran from the car to the stairs that led to our underground house. Once inside the house I felt a little safer. That is, until the lights went out. When the lights go out in an underground house, it gets pretty dark. About that time, sparks started flying off of the metal post in the middle of the living room.

By this time I was really scared and I don't think I was the only one. The lightning was so close you could hear it the moment it hit the ground. I had to go to the bathroom. So I groped my way into the bathroom. Actually, I felt a little safer in there since there were no metal posts in the bathroom.

While I was sitting there, there was another hit of lightning and sparks started flying off of the metal pipes underneath the sink, which was only inches away. I thought I was going to be dead soon. I ran out screaming with my pants half way up. It was then that the three of us decided it was safer in the car with Daddy and Mama.

The storm soon ended and my heart rate returned to normal. The calm aftermath of an Arizona thunderstorm is beautiful to behold. The clouds parted their ways allowing the sun and the blue sky to reappear. Water rushed down the small hills, flooding the gullies that emptied into nearby ponds. The scent of fresh air just after a rain was heavenly.

I learned that day, the fears and joys of the Arizona thunder storm.

LINDA'S STORIES

The Wood Pile:

Daddy had this gigantic wood pile near our house. Sometimes men would come over and help chop the wood. On this particular day a man came to help.

Mama said, "Linda, go show this man where Daddy is. He's out by the wood pile."

I didn't like him so I didn't want to show him. I was six or seven years old. I thought if I can find Daddy, why can't he. He is a grown man. But I had to show him, anyway.

As we started to the wood pile, he picked me up and was carrying me. I was already mad and I didn't want him to touch me, let alone carry me.

He wouldn't put me down. I saw that the back of his collar hanging out a little. I thought, I'll spit down his neck, then he'll put me down. So I did! I spit down his neck. He looked at me, but didn't say a word. Then he put me down real fast.

I showed him where Daddy was, then ran back to the house. I was afraid I was going to get into big trouble for this one, but I guess the man didn't say anything to Daddy and I sure wasn't going to say anything.

The Christmas Check:

One Christmas time, Mama kept telling us, "Don't expect anything for Christmas. Daddy hasn't gotten paid for the last job he did." I was pretty sad because I knew if Mama said that, she was not fooling us.

The day before Christmas, she stood by the mail box waiting for the mailman, hoping and praying that the check would be there. Time went by and finally the mailman came about one o'clock. He handed Mama the mail and she quickly looked through it.

Then we heard her scream, "It came! Go get you shoes and sox on. We're all going shopping!"

I was so happy. I was going to get presents for Christmas! It took us all about two seconds to get out shoes and sox on, and we all ran and piled into our old car.

When we got to the five and dime store, Mama gave us each a whole five dollar bill and said, "Now that is all you can have.

Make sure that you buy a present for everyone." There are ten people in our family and I was supposed to buy nine presents with five dollars???

It seemed as if I shopped for hours just to find the right gift for the right person for the right price. Yep! We all did it by the time we the stores closed. I don't remember what I got that Christmas, but I do remember how happy I was to be with my family and feel so good inside.

Story time:

In the winter time when it got dark out side early and it wasn't time to go to bed yet. After supper, Daddy would build a big fire in the fireplace. We would all sit around it with our pillows and blankets. Then Daddy would tell us stories. Sometimes the stories were funny and sometimes serious, but every story had a moral to teach us something about living right. I always felt that most loved and secure at these times.

Before I would go to bed, Daddy would give me a big bear hug and say, "I am the biggest and you are the littlest. I love you so much. We need to have a littlest one in our family."

I was so happy to be the littlest one in the family.

Playtime:

One of my most favorite things to do was to swing on the wooden swing in the big walnut tree behind the house. I felt so free when I would go as high as the swing would allow. If Mama needed to find me, I was usually swinging under the tree.

Summer time was the best fun. John, Merri Lou and I loved to go "swimming". This had to be done in a fifty gallon barrel, one at a time, in the front yard so Mama could watch us.

We loved to play cowboys and Indians in the afternoons. When we would get tired of that, we would play house if we could talk John into it. Most of the time we could if we promised him one thing or another. I always had fun playing with my brothers and sisters, I have so many of them!

Time With Mama:

When all of my brothers and sisters were at school and I was home alone with Mama was the best of all. She had to make twelve loaves of bread every other day for us. I would watch her pour in each ingredient, then stir it together. When it was time to knead the bread, she would pinch off a piece of dough the size needed for one loaf of bread and tell me it was mine to knead. She would show me exactly how to do this. I thought I was doing pretty good. She would squeeze it to see if I had gotten it smooth enough. If I didn't, I had to keep kneading it until it was smooth enough. My loaf was always put into it own special pan and baked with the rest of the bread.

Mama also taught me how to sew before I went to school. I felt I was so big because I could use her sewing machine. I made lots of handkerchiefs and skirts for my dolls. I loved to sew and learn how to do more.

I am so grateful to my mother for teaching me to sew and cook.

Time with Daddy:

It seemed as if every time Daddy went outside to do something, he would say, "Linda, come go with me."

Most of the time I liked to help Daddy, but sometimes (when I was little) he would step on me if I was in his way. I learned very fast to stay out of his way, and yet try to help in the best way I could.

Daddy always talked with us to teach us right from wrong. Most of all I remember his big giant loving hugs and the soft skin on his face.

Chapter Fifty-two

TIMES AND SEASONS

Up in the foothills in the Mother Load country, near the little town of Plymouth, there is a beautiful ranch called the Steiner Ranch. There were some 160 acres of rolling hills and scrub oak, some tall pine trees, and here and there were several small springs. It was a beautiful place to go on an overnight picnic or an all day outing.

Walt Steiner and his wife lived in a big house that he and she had built themselves out of the native rock that was on the place. They were two of the most outstanding people that I have ever been acquainted with.

Walt had worked in the oil fields in the southern part of California. He saved his money and invested it in property down there. He and his first wife had two boys just one year apart. During World War II both of them were drafted into the army and were sent over seas to fight. They were in two different units. Walt would hear from both of them from time to time.

Then, one day he got a letter stating that one of his boys was killed in action. A week later, he got another letter. The other boy was killed in action, also.

Walt and his wife had just settled down after this double whammy that they had experienced, when his wife was killed in a bad car wreck.

Now Walt was left all alone. His family was all gone. It was a real blow to him. So he decided to sell off everything and just move to get away.

He went up to the little town of Plymouth and started in all over again. He bought this 160 acre ranch that was pretty well run down. All it had on it was a little shack and there was a fence around it. He kept himself busy from morning till night, but he was still lonely and grieving over his lost ones.

Well, one day he met a local school teacher. She had never been married before. They hit if off pretty good together and soon they were married. She quit teaching and the two of them started to build this rock house.

But Walt felt there was still something missing, so they adopted a little boy and a few years later they adopted a little girl. When we got acquainted with them their boy was fifteen years old and the girl was about thirteen. They got along so well I was surprised when he told me this story.

One day we were up there with all of our kids on a Saturday outing. That was a fun place to go and all of the kids loved to go there. We were not the only ones who went up there just to have some fun. Walt liked people and he liked to share what he had with other people. He made some picnic tables and some out houses. He made a play ground for children. There was a teeter-totter and some swings for them to play on. It was a fun place to go and Walt and his wife enjoyed having people there.

Our church wanted to hold a big building-fund-raising barbecue and picnic. Walt volunteered to have it at his ranch and to donate the beef. It was to be a pit barbecue. They hoped to have close to 1,000 people there. It was to be held the third weekend in May.

Me 'n Mama were asked if we would organize the preparation of the food for it. Since we had a big family, we knew how to cook for a large crowd of people.

Well, you know how some of these things go if you're in charge. That means that you take up the slack if some one who says he will do something and he forgets or does not show up.

We had a month to get all prepared for this big occasion. Walt had two 1,000 pound steers for the barbecue, but they had to be slaughtered and the meat cut up into fist-sized pieces. I volunteered to do that.

There was a whole lot of things to do that I had never thought of when we started into this project. There was a barbecue pit to dig and line with fire bricks, which Walt and I did. We wanted homemade bread, so Mama made 100 loaves and froze them till we needed them. There were 100 pounds beans to cook and 100 pounds of cabbage to shred, which we did.

That was the biggest project that me 'n Mama ever put on.

Mama sure worked hard and so did I. Of course, we had some other help, too. The barbecue was a real success. There were close to 1,000 people there and we all felt good about what we had done. We had raised the money we needed

But what happened a few days later was unexpected.

Two days after the big barbecue, I wound up in the hospital. The doctor diagnosed me as having a heart attack. I didn't feel all that bad. I was just real tired.

Well, they kept me in there for ten days till I was about to go nuts. I was not allowed to walk or even get out of bed. And I hate to stay in bed, anyway, and this was just like shutting me up in a dungeon as far as I was concerned, and I had to take all of that medicine.

Finally, I was allowed to go home, but I had to stay in bed for a month before I could get up. Mama was feeding me pills three times a day; pills for my heart and tranquilizers. After a week at home I was feeling worse than I did when I went into the hospital.

The doctor told me that I would have to quit my job at the Stockton State Hospital. Working there was really getting to me. So I quit. Things were getting real bad and we were getting more behind all of the time.

Jim and Jerry had just come home from their first year away at college. Both of them were big young men, as strong as bulls. Everybody liked them. It was easy for them to get a job. They both got jobs working at Orvis and Clinger's, the slaughtering and butchering plant. They were willing to work and help out the family as long as I was sick.

After some three weeks in bed, I was feeling worse. I was a-doin' everything that the doctor told me to do, taking all of those different pills. Finally, I figured that what he was having me a-doin' wasn't working. So I decided to be my own doctor.

While Mama was taking the girls some where or other, I got up and went into the bathroom where all of the pills were kept and opened them all up and flushed them all down the toilet. I put on my clothes and sat down in the living room a-lookin' out the window. Then I thought, those empty bottles are still there. Mama could get those prescriptions refilled. So I went in there and got the labels off and destroyed them. About that time, Mama came in the house and saw me with all of my clothes on.

She put her hands on her hips and said, "Well, what is this all about?"

I said, "I am not taking any more of those pills. I have flushed them all down the toilet. Mama, I feel worse now than I did a week ago, and a whole lot worse that I did when I went to the hospital. If I keep this up I will sure enough die. I'm going to be my own doctor from now on. I am going to go and get myself a job a-doin' something, even if it is nothing more than being a night watchman at the slaughter house. I'll admit that I am pretty weak, but I will get better."

It wasn't but a few days after that that I went down to the slaughter house and asked for a job as a night watchman. They knew that I had been out of work for some time and they said that I could go to work for them. All I had to do was to walk around and see that all of the motors were a-runnin' and that no one came in to steal the meat out of the walk-in boxes.

Well, this went on for a week or so and the man that they had salting down the cow hides quit. They asked me if I would do that for them till they could get someone to do it.

Now, this was hard work, a-pullin' those green hides around, but I had all night to do it in. I did a little and rested till I had them all done. Every day I got to feeling a lot better. I was getting my strength back real fast. But the worst thing about it was being up all night. I am just not a night person. Then they started adding more jobs for me to do till I was a-workin' hard most all night. But I didn't mind 'cause I was a-feelin' a lot better.

It was not too long after that, that I was back a-doin' plastering again.

It wasn't till years later that I found what was really wrong with me. I hadn't had a heart attack at all. It was a hiatal hernia that had given me the problems.

In the Bible there is a scripture in Ecclesiastes, Chapter 3, Verse 1 which says, "To everything there is a season, and a time to every purpose under the heaven." We have found it so in our lives.

Daddy was off work for nearly nine months at this time. The medication and type of therapy and counseling he was getting from the doctor was making him sicker, mentally as well as physically.

Jim and Jerry stayed home from school during the 1960 fall semester to help with the finances of taking care of the family. They were willing to help as long as they were needed, but they were anxious to get on with their own lives.

Both of them wanted to go on a full-time mission for our church, but we didn't have the money to send them, so they couldn't go. When it finally looked like Daddy was going to get back his strength and health, Jim decided to go back to BYU for the second semester. Because of his leg problem he knew that he would have to have a good education and make his living with his head instead of his brawn. He was anxious to get going on it.

Jerry liked plastering and working hard so he decided to stay home and go to work with Daddy.

He had met his future wife during his one semester at college and since he couldn't go on a mission, he decided to ask her to marry him. She said yes and they planned for their wedding to be the following March.

That December of 1960 was the last time we were all together as the Walter and Deloris Swan family unit. We had a family group picture taken. It was the last one we had taken before there were changes in our family. It was fifteen years before we were able to get everyone together again for another family group picture.

That Christmas was probably the most joyous one we ever had. Our Christmas tree was loaded with more presents for everybody than it had ever been before. By the first of the New Year we were all looking forward to new beginnings in our lives.

We didn't realize at the time what the impact of our small decisions had made in our lives. Nor did we realize that very soon big and important changes in our lives would be taking place.

Daddy was feeling better and was able to go back to work. Jim was leaving for Provo to go back to BYU. A few months later he left for Texas where he served a two and a half year mission for our church. Jerry was planning for his marriage. Charlotte was in her last year of high school, looking forward to college after her graduation. Carol Ann was in the process of falling in love with the man she married the next year. And the younger children were continuing to grow like weeds. Our "times and seasons" were changing.

Our lives as "me 'n Mama" would soon be over and from then on it would be "me 'n Grandma". We had survived!

The Swan Family
Back row: Carol Ann, Jerry, Jim, Charlotte, Allen
Front row: Merri Lou, Walter, Linda, Deloris, Johnny

AFTERWORD

After fifty-three years of marriage, we have found that we have had too much story to tell to put it all into one book. We are sorry about that, but the book would be too heavy for you to hold if that were the case. If you have found some mistakes in the text, just blame my human frailties. If we didn't get all of your questions answered in this book, we'll try to get it done in the next one.

However, there is one question I'll answer right here. We told you what happened to Daddy's father in this book. You have asked about his mother, also. She married twice again, losing both of her husbands in death. She worked in California until she became of retirement age. Later, she lived out her last years, back down on the old family homestead, the Swan Ranch. Henry and his wife, and Oliver and his wife were living there at the time, also. "Grandy", as we all called her, fell in her bathroom early one morning and broke her hip. She died three months later, on September 7, 1979, never leaving the hospital after her fall. She was eighty-one years old.

We have already begun writing about our lives as Grandpa and Grandma Swan, which we will put into a book we will title, _"me 'n Grandma"_, with the subtitle being _How We Spent Our Kids Inheritance_.

If we're not able to get all of our story in that book, we'll write another one about how we self-published and went about selling _"me 'n Henry"_ in our _One Book Bookstore_, and our other books in our _Other Book Bookstore_ and the publicity it gave us.

When I was putting our book _"me 'n Henry"_ together, I told Daddy that it was like having another baby. It was his dream child and I was doing all the labor. This one has been like having another child, too. But takes teamwork to do it.

He does what he does best, up at our _One Book Bookstore_, while I operate the computer in our office at home. I can do what he can't, and he can do what I can't. And that just about makes the best team there is.